Dominican Republic Travel Guide

DOMINICAN REPUBLIC TRAVEL GUIDE 2025

Discover Local Culture, Adventures, and Unique Experiences

Conor. S. McMillan

Dominican Republic Travel Guide 2025

© 2024 by Conor S. McMillan

All rights reserved. No part of this book may be reproduced, distributed, or transmitted in any form or by any means, including photocopying, recording, or other electronic or mechanical methods, without the prior written permission of the publisher, except in the case of brief quotations embodied in critical reviews and certain other noncommercial uses permitted by copyright law.

Disclaimer: The information in this guide is accurate as of the time of publication. The author and publisher are not responsible for any changes, errors, or omissions. Travelers are advised to verify all information, including travel requirements, safety guidelines, and health advisories, before making travel arrangements. Use of this guide is at your own risk.

Dominican Republic Travel Guide 2025

Dominican Republic Travel Guide 2025

AUTHOR'S NOTE

Thank you for picking up this guide! The Dominican Republic is a place close to my heart, not just for its stunning landscapes and vibrant culture, but for the way it welcomes visitors with open arms. Whether you're seeking adventure, relaxation, or a little bit of both, this guide is designed to help you uncover the best experiences the island has to offer.

As you explore, I encourage you to not only visit the famous spots but also dive deeper into the hidden gems, local traditions, and everyday moments that make this country so unique. I hope that this guide serves as a helpful companion on your journey, giving you the tools to create lasting memories.

Safe travels, and may your time in the Dominican Republic be filled with joy, discovery, and a sense of wonder.

Dominican Republic Travel Guide 2025

TABLE OF CONTENTS

AUTHOR'S NOTE..4
INTRODUCTION..9
   ➤Why Visit the Dominican Republic.....................10
   ➤Language, Currency, and Time Zone..................13
   ➤Best Time to Visit.. 15
   ➤Budgeting and Costs..20
CHAPTER 1: PLANNING YOUR TRIP..................23
   ➤Health and Safety Tips...24
   ➤Navigating Customs and Local Etiquette............ 27
      ★Managing Currency Exchange and Tipping.. 28
CHAPTER 2: GETTING THERE & AROUND.......30
   ➤Getting Around... 33
CHAPTER 3: TOP DESTINATIONS........................ 38
CHAPTER 4: MUST-SEE SITES AND ATTRACTIONS... 45
   ➤Santo Domingo: The Colonial City...................... 46
   ➤Punta Cana: The Beach Paradise......................... 51
   ➤Puerto Plata: History Meets Adventure............... 57
   ➤La Romana & Bayahibe: Cultural and Coastal Bliss.. 65
   ➤Beaches in the Dominican Republic..................... 71
CHAPTER 5: WHERE TO STAY.............................. 85
   ➤Luxury Hotels.. 85
   ➤Mid-Range Hotels..90
   ➤Budget-Friendly Hotels.. 95

★Tips for Booking Accommodations............ 103

CHAPTER 6: NATURE AND OUTDOOR ADVENTURES..105

➢Museums and Historic Sites............................ 113

CHAPTER 7: FESTIVALS AND EVENTS............ 120

➢Markets for Traditional Crafts.......................... 122

➢Live Music and Dance Performances................ 125

CHAPTER 8: FOOD AND DINING....................... 130

➢Dishes to Try First... 130

➢Where to Experience Authentic Dominican Food... 132

➢Must-Visit Food Markets.................................. 136

★Dining Etiquette and Tipping in the Dominican Republic... 139

CHAPTER 9: NIGHTLIFE AND ENTERTAINMENT... 141

➢Top Nightlife Spots.. 141

➢Cultural Performances: Music, Theater, and Dance 147

★Insider Tips for a Night Out.......................... 150

CHAPTER 10: SHOPPING.......................................153

➢Best Shopping Districts: From High-End Malls to Local Markets... 154

★Top Souvenirs to Bring Home..................... 158

Supporting Local Artisans: Best Stores and Cooperatives... 163

CHAPTER 11: SUGGESTED ITINERARIES........167

➢Hidden Gems of the Dominican Republic......... 176

Dominican Republic Travel Guide 2025

  ★Tips for Finding Hidden Gems.................... 184
CHAPTER 12: STAYING SAFE AND HEALTHY..... 187
  ➢Common Tourist Scams and How to Avoid Them.. 188
  ★Health Tips for Coping with the Tropical Climate... 191
CHAPTER 13: LEAVING THE DOMINICAN REPUBLIC..198
  ★Final Tips for Departure............................. 204
CONCLUSION.. 207
NOTES..209

Dominican Republic Travel Guide 2025

Dominican Republic Travel Guide 2025

INTRODUCTION

Welcome to the Dominican Republic

Imagine a place where the ocean sparkles under the sun, the music fills the air, and every moment feels like an invitation to explore. The Dominican Republic—rich in culture, history, and natural beauty—offers just that and more.

This guide is here to be your companion, leading you through the must-see spots and the hidden gems that make this island so unforgettable. Whether you're strolling through the vibrant streets of Santo Domingo or relaxing on a pristine beach in Punta Cana, every corner holds something special.

Dominican Republic Travel Guide 2025

I want you to feel the excitement of discovery, the thrill of unexpected moments, and the joy of connecting with a place so full of life. Let this be the start of your adventure, where the memories you create will be the ones you carry long after you leave.

➢Why Visit the Dominican Republic

The Dominican Republic is a Caribbean gem that offers more than just postcard-perfect beaches. From its rich cultural heritage to thrilling outdoor adventures, this

Dominican Republic Travel Guide 2025

island has something for every traveler. Whether you're seeking relaxation, exploration, or a deep dive into local culture, here are reasons why the Dominican Republic should be on your travel list.

1. Stunning Beaches and Coastal Beauty

The Dominican Republic is home to some of the most beautiful beaches in the Caribbean. Whether you're lounging on the soft sands of Punta Cana or swimming in the crystal-clear waters of Playa Rincón, the island's coastline is a paradise for sun-seekers and water enthusiasts alike. Each beach offers its unique charm, from secluded coves to lively resort areas.

2. Rich History and Colonial Heritage

Step back in time as you explore Santo Domingo, the oldest city in the New World. Wander through the historic Zona Colonial, a UNESCO World Heritage site, where you can visit centuries-old cathedrals, forts, and cobblestone streets. The Dominican Republic's history is woven into its architecture and culture, making it a must-visit for history buffs.

Dominican Republic Travel Guide 2025

3. Thrilling Outdoor Adventures

If you crave adventure, the Dominican Republic is the perfect playground. Hike to breathtaking waterfalls like El Limón, explore the lush rainforests, or go zip-lining through the canopies. From snorkeling in vibrant coral reefs to kitesurfing in Cabarete, the island offers endless opportunities for thrill-seekers.

4. Vibrant Music and Dance

The Dominican Republic is the birthplace of merengue and bachata, and music is woven into the fabric of everyday life. Whether you're at a local festival or a beachside bar, the infectious rhythm of these traditional dances will have you moving your feet in no time. Experiencing the lively music and dance culture is a highlight for many travelers.

5. Warm and Welcoming People

Perhaps one of the most memorable aspects of visiting the Dominican Republic is the warmth of its people. Known for their hospitality and friendliness, Dominicans are proud to share their culture with visitors. From helpful locals guiding you through markets to heartfelt conversations in a local café, you'll feel right at home as soon as you arrive.

These reasons are just the beginning of what the Dominican Republic has to offer. Whether you're a first-time visitor or a seasoned traveler, this Caribbean destination will leave you with memories to last a lifetime.

➤Language, Currency, and Time Zone

When traveling to the Dominican Republic, it's helpful to know a little about the local language and how things work. The official language is Spanish, and while you'll find many people who speak English in tourist areas like resorts or hotels, picking up a few Spanish phrases will go a long way. Even simple greetings like "Hola" (Hello) or "Gracias" (Thank you) can make your interactions warmer and more fun!

Dominican Republic Travel Guide 2025

In terms of money, the official currency is the Dominican Peso (DOP). However, in many tourist hotspots, U.S. dollars are widely accepted, and you'll find ATMs that dispense both pesos and dollars. It's still a good idea to have some local currency for smaller purchases, especially when you're venturing outside of the main tourist zones. Credit cards are also accepted in most hotels and restaurants, but always double-check before making a purchase.

The Dominican Republic is in the Atlantic Standard Time Zone (AST), which is the same as Eastern Standard Time (EST), but they don't observe daylight savings time. So if you're traveling from the U.S. during the winter months, the time will be the same as EST, but in summer, the island will be one hour ahead. It's a good idea to adjust your clocks to make sure you don't miss out on any excursions or dinner reservations!

Dominican Republic Travel Guide 2025

➢Best Time to Visit

While the Dominican Republic is beautiful year-round, certain times are better depending on what you're looking to experience. The best time to visit is during the dry season, which runs from December to April. During these months, you'll enjoy sunny days, clear skies, and warm temperatures—perfect for beach lounging, sightseeing, and outdoor adventures. It's also the peak tourist season, so if you love a lively atmosphere, this is the time to go.

If you prefer fewer crowds and don't mind a little rain, the shoulder seasons—May to June and September to November—offer great weather with fewer tourists. Plus, prices for hotels and flights tend to be a bit lower. Just keep in mind that hurricane season falls between June and November, but the island generally sees more tropical storms than full-blown hurricanes.

Dominican Republic Travel Guide 2025

No matter when you decide to visit, the Dominican Republic is sure to greet you with beautiful weather, warm hospitality, and a rich variety of activities to make your trip unforgettable.

Best times for specific activities in the Dominican Republic:

- **Beach Days and Water Sports**

If your dream vacation involves lounging on beautiful beaches or engaging in water sports like snorkeling, scuba diving, or windsurfing, the dry season (December to April) is your best bet. The weather is perfect for soaking up the sun, and the ocean conditions are ideal for clear underwater visibility.

Best Time: December to April (Dry Season)
Locations: Punta Cana, Playa Rincón, Bávaro Beach, Cabarete (for windsurfing)

- **Hiking and Outdoor Adventures**

For those who love outdoor activities like hiking, zip-lining, and exploring waterfalls, the cooler, drier months of November to March are the most comfortable for trekking through the lush mountains or visiting natural wonders like Pico Duarte and El Limón Waterfall. The landscapes are vibrant, and the weather is not too humid for hiking.

Best Time: November to March
Locations: Jarabacoa (for mountain adventures), Salto de Jimenoa, El Limón Waterfall

- **Cultural Festivals and Events**

The Dominican Republic comes alive with vibrant festivals, music, and dance throughout the year, but the Carnival in February is the most celebrated event. It's an explosion of color, culture, and excitement, especially in Santo Domingo and La Vega. For music lovers, the Merengue Festival, held in July, is also a highlight.

Best Time: February (Carnival), July (Merengue Festival)
Locations: Santo Domingo, La Vega (Carnival); Santo Domingo (Merengue Festival)

Dominican Republic Travel Guide 2025

- **Whale Watching**

One of the most breathtaking natural events in the Dominican Republic is the annual humpback whale migration. From mid-January to mid-March, you can witness these magnificent creatures as they breed and give birth off the coast of the Samaná Peninsula. Several tours are available, offering close encounters with these gentle giants.

Best Time: Mid-January to mid-March
Location: Samaná Peninsula

- **Budget-Friendly Travel**

If you're looking to save on your trip, the off-season (June to November) is when you'll find the best deals on accommodations and activities. Just keep in mind that this is also hurricane season, so it's important to check the weather forecast and be flexible with your plans.

Best Time: June to November
Note: Plan and monitor weather conditions due to hurricane season.

Dominican Republic Travel Guide 2025

- **Birdwatching and Ecotourism**

Nature lovers will enjoy exploring the Dominican Republic's national parks and reserves. The island is home to a wide variety of bird species, including some that are endemic to the region. The best time for birdwatching and ecotourism is during the cooler months of the dry season when the wildlife is most active.

Best Time: December to April
Locations: Los Haitises National Park, Lago Enriquillo, Sierra de Bahoruco National Park

- **Diving and Snorkeling**

For the best underwater experiences, April to August offers calm seas and warm water temperatures. Coral reefs and marine life are vibrant, making it the perfect time to dive or snorkel along the coastlines of places like Sosúa or Bayahibe.

Best Time: April to August
Locations: Sosúa, Bayahibe, Catalina Island

Dominican Republic Travel Guide 2025

By aligning your travel dates with these optimal times for specific activities, you can ensure your trip to the Dominican Republic is filled with unforgettable experiences that match your interests.

➢Budgeting and Costs

When planning a trip to the Dominican Republic, it's always helpful to have an idea of what to budget for daily expenses.

Here's a general breakdown of what you can expect to spend on food, accommodation, and transportation while visiting the island:

- **Food Costs**

Eating out in the Dominican Republic offers options for every budget, whether you're grabbing a quick bite at a local eatery or indulging in fine dining at a beachfront restaurant. For a casual meal at a local spot, expect to pay around $5 to $10 per person, especially if you're enjoying typical Dominican dishes like "sancocho" or "tostones." If you're looking to dine at a mid-range restaurant, meals can range from $15 to $25 per person, depending on the location and type of cuisine. For those looking for a high-end experience, expect to spend $30 to $50 or more for a three-course meal at a fine dining restaurant.

- **Accommodation Costs**

The price of accommodation in the Dominican Republic varies depending on where you stay and the level of comfort you're seeking. Budget travelers can find hostels or budget hotels for as low as $20 to $40 per night, particularly in less touristy areas. Mid-range hotels and boutique stays typically cost between $70 to $150 per night. If you're planning to stay at a luxury resort, particularly in places like Punta Cana or Samaná, prices generally start at $200 per night and can go much higher depending on the resort's amenities and location. All-inclusive resorts may range from $250 to $500 per night, depending on the season and package inclusions.

- **Transportation Costs**

Dominican Republic Travel Guide 2025

Getting around the Dominican Republic can be quite affordable if you use local transportation. Buses or "guaguas" (shared minibusses) are very economical, with fares ranging from $1 to $3 depending on the distance. For a more comfortable ride, long-distance buses like Caribe Tours or Metro typically cost around $10 to $15 for a trip between major cities. Taxis in tourist areas can be pricier, with short trips starting around $10 to $20, so it's always a good idea to agree on the fare before hopping in. Ride-sharing apps like Uber are available in some cities and tend to be cheaper, with fares averaging around $5 to $15 for most trips. Renting a car will cost you around $40 to $70 per day, depending on the type of vehicle and rental company.

This should give you a good sense of how to plan your budget for a trip to the Dominican Republic. Whether you're looking to splurge or keep things affordable, the island has something to suit every travel style.

Dominican Republic Travel Guide 2025

CHAPTER 1:
PLANNING YOUR TRIP

- **Visa Requirements for Tourists**

Traveling to the Dominican Republic is pretty straightforward for many tourists, especially if you're from the U.S., Canada, or most European countries. For short stays (usually up to 30 days), many visitors don't need a visa. Instead, you'll be required to purchase a tourist card either online before your trip or upon arrival at the airport. This costs around $10. However, if you're planning a longer stay or you're from a country that does

Dominican Republic Travel Guide 2025

require a visa, it's best to check with your local Dominican embassy or consulate to confirm the entry requirements. For travelers who do need a visa, the application process typically involves submitting your passport, a completed application form, and a visa fee. Always apply a few weeks ahead of time to avoid any last-minute stress.

➤Health and Safety Tips

When traveling to the Dominican Republic, it's important to keep a few health and safety precautions in mind:

- **Vaccinations**: While no specific vaccines are required for entry, it's a good idea to be up-to-date on routine vaccines like hepatitis A, typhoid, and tetanus. If you're planning to venture into more rural areas, you may want to consult your doctor about malaria prevention.

- **Health Insurance**: Make sure your health insurance covers international travel, or consider purchasing a short-term travel health insurance policy. Medical care in tourist areas is generally good, but private hospitals can be expensive without coverage.
- **Staying Safe in Urban Areas**: Like any country, the Dominican Republic has its share of petty crime, particularly in large cities. Be mindful of your surroundings, avoid displaying valuables, and stick to well-lit, populated areas at night. In tourist-heavy spots, it's always a good idea to stay in groups or use trusted transportation services.

Packing Checklist for Various Activities

Here's a helpful packing checklist depending on the type of activities you're planning:

Beach Vacation:
- Lightweight clothing (shorts, swimsuits, flip-flops)

Dominican Republic Travel Guide 2025

- Sunblock, sunglasses, and a hat
- Snorkeling gear (optional)
- A waterproof phone case and beach bag
- Light jacket or sweater for cooler evenings

Eco-Tourism Adventures:

- Comfortable hiking shoes or sandals
- Reusable water bottles and eco-friendly toiletries
- Bug spray with DEET (mosquitoes can be a concern)
- Long-sleeve, light clothing for sun protection
- A small daypack for hiking essentials

City Exploration:

- Casual, comfortable walking shoes
- A cross-body bag or backpack for city strolling
- Portable charger for your phone or camera
- Dressier outfit if you plan on dining in upscale restaurants
- Local guidebooks or apps to enhance your sightseeing experience

Dominican Republic Travel Guide 2025

➤Navigating Customs and Local Etiquette

Dominicans are warm, friendly people, and as a traveler, you'll quickly pick up on their laid-back attitude and hospitality. However, it's important to respect local customs and cultural norms:

- **Greetings**: When meeting someone, a handshake or a kiss on the cheek (if you're familiar) is common. Always greet with a friendly "¡Hola!" or "Buenos días."
- **Dress Code**: Casual is fine in most places, but if you're visiting churches or government buildings, it's polite to dress modestly (avoid shorts and sleeveless tops).
- **Tipping**: It's customary to tip around 10% at restaurants, although many places include a service charge on the bill. Always check the bill before tipping extra.

- **Local Manners**: It's always appreciated when travelers try to speak a bit of Spanish, even just a few phrases. Simple words like "gracias" (thank you) or "por favor" (please) go a long way. Also, avoid discussing politics, especially around sensitive topics.

★ Managing Currency Exchange and Tipping

The local currency is the Dominican Peso (DOP), though U.S. dollars are widely accepted in many tourist areas. Here's how to handle your money while traveling:

Currency Exchange: ATMs are readily available in cities and resort areas, and they offer some of the best exchange rates. It's best to withdraw pesos once you arrive instead of exchanging currency at the airport, where rates can be unfavorable. If you need to exchange cash, visit a reputable exchange office (casa de cambio) or a bank.

- **ATMs**: Use ATMs in well-lit, secure areas, preferably those attached to a bank. If you're staying at a resort, they often have ATMs on-site for convenience.

- **Tipping**: In addition to restaurants, it's polite to tip service workers such as bellhops (around $1-2 USD per bag) and housekeeping (around $1-2 USD per day). For taxi rides, rounding up the fare or tipping $1-2 USD is appreciated but not mandatory.

These practical tips should help you feel well-prepared for your trip to the Dominican Republic, whether you're planning a relaxing beach getaway or a city adventure.

Dominican Republic Travel Guide 2025

CHAPTER 2: GETTING THERE & AROUND

Before you can start soaking up the sun and exploring the vibrant culture of the Dominican Republic, you'll need to figure out the best way to get here. Luckily, whether you're flying in from North America, Europe, or anywhere else, getting to this Caribbean paradise is pretty straightforward. With multiple international airports—like Punta Cana, Santo Domingo, and Puerto Plata—you'll likely find a direct flight from most major

Dominican Republic Travel Guide 2025

cities. If you're traveling from nearby islands, ferry services are also available.

Let's take a closer look at how you can make your way to the Dominican Republic, stress-free and ready for adventure.

Traveling to the Dominican Republic is straightforward, with several options depending on where you're coming from. The country is well-connected by international flights, making it accessible from various parts of the world.

By Air: The easiest way to reach the Dominican Republic is by air. The country has several international airports, with the three main ones being:

1. **Punta Cana International Airport (PUJ):** Located on the eastern coast, this is the busiest airport in the country and serves as the primary gateway for tourists heading to the beach resorts in Punta Cana, Bávaro, and nearby areas.

2. **Las Américas International Airport (SDQ):** Just outside the capital, Santo Domingo, this airport is ideal for travelers visiting the city or exploring the southern and central regions of the country.

3. **Gregorio Luperón International Airport (POP):** Located near Puerto Plata on the northern coast, this airport is best for travelers heading to Puerto Plata, Sosúa, or Cabarete.

Direct Flights: The Dominican Republic is served by direct flights from major cities in the United States, Canada, Europe, and parts of Latin America. Airlines such as American Airlines, JetBlue, Delta, and British Airways offer regular flights. Flight times from popular hubs:

From New York: About 4 hours.

From Miami: Just over 2 hours.

From London: Around 9 hours.

Travel by Sea: For those seeking a more leisurely arrival, cruise ships frequently stop at Dominican ports

Dominican Republic Travel Guide 2025

like Amber Cove near Puerto Plata or La Romana. These ports are popular stops for Caribbean cruises.

Entry Requirements: For most travelers, including those from the U.S., Canada, and Europe, no visa is required for short stays (up to 30 days). You will need to purchase a tourist card for $10, which can be done online before your trip or upon arrival at the airport.

With plenty of flight options and well-connected airports, getting to the Dominican Republic is a breeze, setting the stage for your adventure ahead.

➤Getting Around

When you land in the Dominican Republic, one of the first things you'll need to figure out is how to get around, whether you're headed straight for the beach or exploring the bustling streets of Santo Domingo. Whether you're a fan of public transportation or prefer the comfort of private shuttles, there's a travel option to suit every style and budget.

From hopping in a local guagua to renting your car, let's break down all the ways to get from A to B on this beautiful island.

Traveling within the Dominican Republic is flexible, with several options available depending on your budget and comfort preferences.

Here's a breakdown of the most common ways to get around:

1. **Taxis and Ride-Sharing (Uber):** Taxis are widely available, especially in tourist areas like Punta Cana, Santo Domingo, and Puerto Plata. It's important to agree on the fare before starting your trip, as most taxis don't use meters. Typical taxi fares range from $10 to $30 for short trips, depending on the distance.

In larger cities like Santo Domingo and Santiago, Uber operates reliably and is often cheaper than traditional taxis. You can request a ride directly through the app, with fares displayed upfront. Expect to pay $5 to $20 for most Uber rides within these cities.

2. **Public Buses (Guaguas and OMSA):** For a budget-friendly option, guaguas (local mini buses) are a popular way to travel between cities and towns. They are affordable, with fares typically ranging from $1 to $3. However, they can be crowded, and the routes aren't always fixed, so they're best suited for adventurous travelers.

For longer trips between cities, comfortable coach buses like Caribe Tours and Metro are available. These buses offer air conditioning and assigned seating, making them a convenient option for cross-country travel. Fares for these services range from $5 to $15, depending on the distance.

3. **Renting a Car:** If you prefer to explore at your own pace, renting a car is a good option. Car rental prices typically range from $40 to $70 per day, depending on the vehicle and rental

company. Most major rental companies, such as Hertz, Avis, and Budget, have offices at the main airports.

Driving Tips: While major highways are in decent condition, some rural roads may be poorly maintained with potholes or unclear signage. Defensive driving is recommended, especially when sharing the road with motorcycles. Parking is generally easy to find in tourist areas but may be limited in city centers.

4. **Domestic Flights:** If you're short on time and want to visit multiple regions, domestic flights are an option. Carriers like Air Century offer flights between Santo Domingo, Punta Cana, and Santiago. Flights are relatively short, typically under an hour, with fares ranging from $60 to $120 one-way.

5. **Shared Taxis (Conchos):** In cities like Santo Domingo and Santiago, conchos (shared taxis) operate on specific routes, picking up and dropping off passengers along the way. They are

very affordable, usually costing around $1 per ride, but can be cramped since you'll be sharing the space with other passengers. They are best for short trips within the city.

6. **Private Transfers:** For travelers who want comfort and convenience, private transfers are available for airport pickups and day trips. Many hotels and tour companies offer these services, which typically cost $50 to $150 depending on the distance and vehicle type.

With various transportation options to choose from, getting around the Dominican Republic can be both easy and affordable, whether you're sticking to the cities or venturing off to explore the countryside.

CHAPTER 3: TOP DESTINATIONS

The Dominican Republic offers a variety of destinations, each with its charm. From vibrant cities to pristine beaches, there's something for every type of traveler. Here's a breakdown of must-see attractions in some of the most popular areas, along with practical tips on getting there and making the most of your visit.

Whether you're visiting the beaches, history, or natural wonders, the Dominican Republic offers something for every traveler. Below are the top destinations you won't want to miss, each with its unique charm and experiences.

1. Santo Domingo – The Historic Heart

As the oldest city in the New World, Santo Domingo is the cultural and historical hub of the Dominican Republic. Wander through the Zona Colonial, a UNESCO World Heritage Site, where you'll find some

Dominican Republic Travel Guide 2025

of the most significant landmarks in the Americas, like the Catedral Primada de América.

Top Attractions:
- Zona Colonial (Cultural District, entry free to explore the area)
- Museo de las Casas Reales ($3 USD entry)
- National Palace (Government building, guided tours available)

Local Experiences:
- Stroll down El Conde Street for shopping and street food.
- Visit in July/August for the Santo Domingo Merengue Festival.

Getting There: Fly into Las Américas International Airport (SDQ), then take a taxi or Uber ($15-$25) to the city center.

2. Punta Cana – Beach Paradise

Dominican Republic Travel Guide 2025

Punta Cana is all about luxury resorts, pristine beaches, and water sports. With its turquoise waters and white sands, Bávaro Beach is the star attraction, perfect for swimming, snorkeling, or just relaxing under the sun.

Top Attractions:
- Bávaro Beach (Free access, water sports rental available)
- Hoyo Azul ($70 entry for Scape Park)

Local Experiences:
- Take a catamaran cruise to Saona Island for a day of snorkeling and exploring ($50-$80 for tours).

Dominican Republic Travel Guide 2025

- Explore the Indigenous Eyes Ecological Reserve.

Getting There: Fly into Punta Cana International Airport (PUJ), then take a shuttle or taxi to your resort (around $20-$40).

3. Puerto Plata – Adventure and History Combined

Puerto Plata blends history with adventure, offering everything from colonial forts to adventure parks. Start with a cable car ride up Mount Isabel de Torres for sweeping views of the region, then dive into history at Fortaleza San Felipe, a 16th-century fortress.

Top Attractions:
- Mount Isabel de Torres ($10 for cable car)
- Fortaleza San Felipe ($2 USD entry)

Local Experiences:
- Hike through the 27 Waterfalls of Damajagua, a series of natural waterfalls you can jump and slide down ($13-$30 for tours).

- Visit Amber Cove Cruise Port, a modern cruise port with zip-lining and shopping.

Getting There: Fly into Gregorio Luperón International Airport (POP), then take a taxi into town ($20).

4. Samaná Peninsula – Nature and Ecotourism Haven

The Samaná Peninsula is where nature lovers will feel at home. Known for its untouched beauty, you can hike to the stunning El Limón Waterfall or enjoy whale watching in Samaná Bay (January-March).

Top Attractions:
- El Limón Waterfall ($20 for guided horseback tours)
- Cayo Levantado (Day trips available, $20 for ferry)

Local Experiences:
- Whale-watching tours in Samaná Bay ($50-$80, January-March).
- Enjoy secluded beaches like Playa Rincón.

Dominican Republic Travel Guide 2025

Getting There: Buses from Santo Domingo are available through Caribe Tours ($10-$12) or drive 3 hours from the capital.

5. La Romana – Culture and Relaxation

La Romana is home to Altos de Chavón, a replica Mediterranean village perched above the Chavón River, offering art galleries and stunning views. From here, you can also take day trips to the picture-perfect Isla Saona.

Top Attractions:
- Altos de Chavón ($5 USD entry)
- Isla Saona (Day trips $50-$80)

Local Experiences:
- Visit Altos de Chavón's amphitheater for concerts and events.
- Take a scenic river cruise along the Chavón River.

Getting There: From Punta Cana, drive 45 minutes or take a bus to La Romana ($10).

How to Plan Your Trip

- **Beach Lovers:** Punta Cana and Puerto Plata should be at the top of your list for beautiful coastlines and resort stays.
- **History Buffs:** Start in Santo Domingo to explore the colonial past, then move to Puerto Plata for a deeper dive into the country's rich history.
- **Nature Enthusiasts:** Head to the Samaná Peninsula for eco-tourism, waterfalls, and whale watching.
- **Cultural Explorers**: La Romana offers a mix of art, history, and relaxation, perfect for travelers looking for more than just beaches.

Final Tips for Visiting

- **Best Times to Visit**: The Dominican Republic is great year-round, but for fewer crowds and more pleasant weather, visit between November and March.
- **Avoid Crowds:** Popular spots like Bávaro Beach and Isla Saona can get busy on weekends. Try

Dominican Republic Travel Guide 2025

visiting early in the morning or during weekdays for a more relaxed experience.

Dominican Republic Travel Guide 2025

CHAPTER 4: MUST-SEE SITES AND ATTRACTIONS

When visiting the Dominican Republic, each destination offers its own unique experiences, from historical landmarks to natural wonders. This chapter breaks down the top attractions, providing essential information for each one: what to expect, how to get there, nearby sights, and helpful tips to make the most of your visit.

Dominican Republic Travel Guide 2025

We've also included some hidden gems that you won't want to miss.

➢Santo Domingo: The Colonial City

1. Zona Colonial (Colonial Zone)

Overview:

This UNESCO World Heritage Site is the heart of Santo Domingo's history. It features stunning architecture from the 16th century, including the first cathedral in the Americas, Catedral Primada de América. Visitors can stroll along cobblestone streets lined with colonial-era buildings, museums, and lively squares.

SCAN TO ACCESS ZONA COLONIAL

Dominican Republic Travel Guide 2025

What to Expect:

The Colonial Zone offers a mix of historical sights, quaint cafes, and vibrant street life. Key spots to visit include, Catedral Primada de América, and Fortaleza Ozama, a 16th-century fortress. You'll also find plenty of local shops and markets selling handcrafted items.

Practical Info:

Location: F4F8+3F2, Santo Domingo 10210, Dominican Republic

Opening Hours: Most landmarks open daily from 9 AM to 5 PM.

Fees: Entrance fees range from $2 to $5 for individual attractions.

Nearby Attractions: Visit the Museo de las Casas Reales or enjoy a meal in Plaza de España with a view of Santo Domingo Malecon.

Hidden Gem:

Tres Ojos National Park is just a short drive away. This natural limestone cave system with crystal-clear lagoons is a perfect quiet escape from the bustling city.

2. Catedral Primada de América

Overview:

This is the oldest cathedral in the Americas, built between 1514 and 1541. Its Gothic and Renaissance architecture has stood the test of time, making it a must-see for history buffs.

SCAN TO ACCESS CATEDRAL PRIMADA DE AMÉRICA

What to Expect:

Dominican Republic Travel Guide 2025

Inside, you'll find stunning artwork, religious artifacts, and chapels dedicated to various saints. The surrounding Parque Colón offers a peaceful place to relax after your visit.

Practical Info:
Location: F4F8+698, C. Isabel La Católica, Santo Domingo 10210, Dominican Republic
Contact Info: +1 809-682-3848
Opening Hours: Daily from 9 AM to 4 PM.
Fees: $2 for entry.
Nearby Attractions: Walk to Amber World Museum, Plaza de España, or enjoy coffee at a nearby café.

Hidden Gem:
Just a 5-minute walk away, visit the Panteón Nacional, where Dominican national heroes are buried. It's a quiet, reverent site.

3. Faro a Colón (Columbus Lighthouse)

Overview:

Dominican Republic Travel Guide 2025

The Faro a Colón, or Columbus Lighthouse, is a massive cross-shaped monument built to honor Christopher Columbus. This striking structure houses a museum with artifacts related to Columbus and his voyages, and it is said to hold his remains. The lighthouse itself is a mix of history and modern architecture, making it one of the most unique landmarks in Santo Domingo.

SCAN TO ACCESS FARO A COLÓN (COLUMBUS LIGHTHOUSE)

What to Expect:

Inside, visitors can explore a series of exhibits that detail the history of Columbus' expeditions, as well as the impact of colonization on the Americas. At night, the lighthouse beams light in the shape of a cross, a spectacular sight. The surrounding park is a peaceful place to walk around and enjoy the views.

Dominican Republic Travel Guide 2025

Practical Info:

Location: Av Mirador del Este, Santo Domingo Este 11604, Dominican Republic

Contact Info: +1 809-591-4844

Opening Hours: Tuesday to Sunday, 9 AM to 5 PM

Fees: $2 USD entry

Nearby Attractions: The Dominican Republic National Aquarium and Parque Los Tres Ojos also known The Three Eyes National Park (a network of underground lakes and caves) are both nearby, offering more opportunities for exploration after your visit.

Hidden Gem:

Don't miss the Museo del Hombre Dominicano nearby, which offers a deep dive into the indigenous and African influences that have shaped the Dominican Republic's culture.

➢Punta Cana: The Beach Paradise

4. Bávaro Beach

Dominican Republic Travel Guide 2025

Bávaro Beach

Overview:

Bávaro Beach is known for its white sand and turquoise waters, making it one of the top beach destinations in the Caribbean. It's perfect for sunbathing, swimming, or trying out water sports like parasailing and snorkeling.

SCAN TO ACCESS BÁVARO BEACH

What to Expect:

Along the shore, you'll find all-inclusive resorts offering easy access to the beach, water sports rentals, and beachfront dining. It's lively but spacious enough to find quiet areas to relax.

Practical Info:

Location: 23000, Dominican Republic

Activities: Water sports such as jet skiing, scuba diving, and glass-bottom boat tours are readily available.

Nearby Attractions: A short boat trip takes you to Isla Saona, a pristine island ideal for a day trip. Also, check out Manati Park for wildlife encounters.

Hidden Gem:

If you're looking for something more secluded, head to Macao Beach, a lesser-known spot about 30 minutes away by car. It's popular with surfers and offers a more rugged, untouched feel.

5. Hoyo Azul (Blue Hole)

Dominican Republic Travel Guide 2025

Overview:

This hidden lagoon at the base of a 200-foot cliff offers crystal-clear turquoise water, making it a popular spot for nature lovers and adventure seekers.

SCAN TO ACCESS
HOYO AZUL
(BLUE HOLE)

What to Expect:

Dominican Republic Travel Guide 2025

You can reach Hoyo Azul via a short, scenic hike through the forest. Once there, take a refreshing swim in the cool, clear waters.

Practical Info:

Location: 23000 Punta Cana, Dominican Republic

Opening Hours: 9 AM to 5 PM daily.

Fees: Entrance to Scape Park is $69, which includes access to Hoyo Azul and other attractions.

Nearby Attractions: Scape Park also offers zip lining, cave tours, and cultural exhibits.

Hidden Gem:

While at Scape Park, visit Cenote Las Ondas, another beautiful water feature tucked within the natural landscape.

6. Indigenous Eyes Ecological Park

Overview:

A private reserve with twelve freshwater lagoons, five of which are open for swimming, Indigenous Eyes Ecological Park offers a peaceful escape into nature.

What to Expect:

Dominican Republic Travel Guide 2025

Take a self-guided tour along well-marked trails, enjoy a swim in the lagoons, or learn about the local flora and fauna. It's a great spot for families and nature enthusiasts.

SCAN TO ACCESS INDIGENOUS EYES ECOLOGICAL PARK

Practical Info:

Location: GJ7C+F8Q, Punta Cana 23000, Dominican Republic

Contact Info : +1 809-959-9221

Opening Hours: 8 AM to 5 PM daily.

Fees: $50 for entrance.

Nearby Attractions: Visit Marina Cap Cana for a relaxing boat tour or waterfront dining experience.

Hidden Gem:

Explore the Puntacana Village, a charming shopping and dining area near the park.

Dominican Republic Travel Guide 2025

➢Puerto Plata: History Meets Adventure

7. Mount Isabel de Torres

Overview:

Rising 2,600 feet above Puerto Plata, Mount Isabel de Torres offers breathtaking views of the coastline. Visitors can take a cable car ride to the top, where they'll find a botanical garden and a giant Christ the Redeemer statue overlooking the city.

What to Expect:

Dominican Republic Travel Guide 2025

SCAN TO ACCESS MOUNT ISABEL DE TORRES

The ride up the mountain offers stunning panoramic views, and at the top, you can wander through beautiful gardens. It's a peaceful retreat from the city below, ideal for taking photos and enjoying nature.

Practical Info:

Location: 57000, Dominican Republic

Opening Hours: Daily from 8 AM to 5 PM.

Fees: $10 for the round-trip cable car ride.

Nearby Attractions: After visiting the mountain, stop by Fortaleza San Felipe, a well-preserved fortress with ocean views.

Hidden Gem:

Dominican Republic Travel Guide 2025

Take a hike to the nearby 27 Charcos de Damajagua (27 Waterfalls), where you can slide and jump into natural pools. It's an exhilarating adventure for those who love the outdoors.

Samaná Peninsula: Nature and Tranquility

8. El Limón Waterfall

Overview:

El Limón Waterfall is a majestic 130-foot cascade hidden within the lush rainforest of the Samaná Peninsula. It's a must-see for nature lovers and those looking to escape the more crowded tourist areas.

SCAN TO ACCESS
EL LIMÓN
WATERFALL

What to Expect:

The hike to the waterfall is about 1.5 miles, and visitors can either walk or ride horses to reach the site. Once there, you can swim in the natural pool at the base of the falls.

Practical Info:
Location: El Limón 32000, Dominican Republic
Contact Info: +1 829-465-8614
Opening Hours: Open year-round during daylight hours.
Fees: Entrance fees range from $5 to $10, with an additional cost for horse rentals.
Nearby Attractions: Combine your visit with a trip to Playa Rincón, one of the most beautiful and remote beaches in the Dominican Republic.

Hidden Gem:
For a unique experience, book a whale-watching tour from January to March, when humpback whales migrate through the Samaná Bay.

9. Fortaleza de San Felipe

Dominican Republic Travel Guide 2025

Fortaleza de San Felipe

Overview:

Built-in the 16th century to protect Puerto Plata from pirates, Fort San Felipe is one of the oldest fortresses in the New World and offers a fascinating glimpse into the island's military history.

SCAN TO ACCESS FORTALEZA DE SAN FELIPE

What to Expect:

Dominican Republic Travel Guide 2025

Visitors can tour the well-preserved fort, learn about its role in colonial defense, and enjoy scenic views of the Atlantic Ocean.

Practical Info:

Location: Puerto Plata Harbor LightHouse, Parque San Felipe, Av. Gral. Gregorio Luperón, Puerto Plata 57000, Dominican Republic

Contact Info: +1 809-261-1911

Opening Hours: 9 AM to 5 PM daily.

Fees: $2 entry.

Nearby Attractions: Visit the Amber Museum (Museo del Ámbar Dominicano), located in a beautiful Victorian mansion, to learn about the island's rich history in amber mining.

Hidden Gem:

Stroll along the Puerto Plata Malecón for a seaside walk with views of the harbor and the fortress.

10. Amber Museum (Museo del Ámbar Dominicano)

Dominican Republic Travel Guide 2025

Overview:

The Amber Museum houses an impressive collection of Dominican amber, which often contains prehistoric plant and animal inclusions, making it a true treasure for history and science enthusiasts.

SCAN TO ACCESS AMBER MUSEUM (MUSEO DEL ÁMBAR DOMINICANO)

What to Expect:

Take a guided tour of the museum to learn about the formation and significance of amber in the region. The museum shop also offers a chance to purchase unique amber jewelry.

Practical Info:
Location: Calle Duarte. 59 con, C. Emilio Prud'Homme, Puerto Plata 57000, Dominican Republic
Contact Info: +1 809-734-2599
Opening Hours: 8 AM to 4 PM, Monday to Saturday.
Fees: $5 entry.
Nearby Attractions: Visit Fortaleza San Felipe and the iconic Cathedral of St. Philip the Apostle (Catedral de San Felipe Apóstol).

Hidden Gem:
Check out House of Culture (Casa de Cultura), a lesser-known cultural center offering art exhibits and performances, just a short walk from the museum.

Dominican Republic Travel Guide 2025

➢La Romana & Bayahibe: Cultural and Coastal Bliss

11. Altos de Chavón

Overview:

This replica of a 16th-century Mediterranean village is perched above the Chavón River and offers a glimpse into Dominican art, history, and culture. Altos de Chavón is also home to an amphitheater that hosts concerts and events, as well as a charming artists' village.

SCAN TO ACCESS ALTOS DE CHAVÓN

What to Expect:

Explore cobblestone streets, visit the archaeological museum, and discover local art galleries. The amphitheater has hosted world-famous artists like Frank

Dominican Republic Travel Guide 2025

Sinatra, and if you're lucky, your visit might coincide with a live performance.

Practical Info:

Location: Casa de Campo Resort and Villas, La Romana 22000, Dominican Republic

Contact Info: +1 809-523-3318

Opening Hours: Open daily, 9 AM to 6 PM.

Fees: $10 entrance fee.

Nearby Attractions: After exploring Altos de Chavón, take a boat to Isla Catalina, known for its excellent snorkeling and diving spots.

Hidden Gem:

Check out Cueva de las Maravillas (Cave of Wonders) located between La Romana and San Pedro de Macorís. This cave system features ancient Taino drawings and is illuminated for a unique underground tour.

12. Isla Catalina

Overview:

Dominican Republic Travel Guide 2025

This small island off the coast of La Romana is known for its crystal-clear waters and rich coral reefs, making it one of the best snorkeling and diving spots in the Dominican Republic. It's a popular day trip for both tourists and locals.

SCAN TO ACCESS ISLA CATALINA

What to Expect:

Visitors can enjoy pristine beaches, snorkeling, scuba diving, or simply relaxing on the sand. The marine life here is abundant, with colorful coral gardens and a variety of fish species to see. Dive operators often offer excursions to explore the underwater life around the island.

Practical Info:

Location: 22000, Dominican Republic

Dominican Republic Travel Guide 2025

Activities: Snorkeling and scuba diving tours typically range from $50 to $100, depending on the provider and equipment rental.

Nearby Attractions: After returning to La Romana, explore Cueva de las Maravillas (Cave of Wonders) for a fascinating underground experience.

Hidden Gem:

For a quieter, more isolated spot, visit the back side of Isla Catalina, where the crowds thin out, and you can enjoy the tranquility of the island.

13. Cueva de las Maravillas (Cave of Wonders)

Dominican Republic Travel Guide 2025

Overview:

Cueva de las Maravillas is an impressive underground cave system located between La Romana and San Pedro de Macorís. It's famous for its ancient Taino petroglyphs and modern lighting that enhances the dramatic rock formations.

SCAN TO ACCESS CUEVA DE LAS MARAVILLAS (CAVE OF WONDERS)

What to Expect:

Take a guided tour to see the petroglyphs and learn about the Taino people who inhabited the island long before European colonization. The cave is well-lit and has smooth pathways, making it accessible to most visitors. You'll also encounter stalactites, stalagmites, and underground lakes.

Practical Info:

Location: Carretera La Romana - San Pedro de Macoris - KM 16, Autovía del Este, Dominican Republic

Dominican Republic Travel Guide 2025

Contact Info: +1 809-951-9009

Opening Hours: Daily from 9 AM to 5 PM

Fees: $6 for entry

Nearby Attractions: Take a boat ride to Isla Saona for a beach escape.

Hidden Gem:

For a unique souvenir, stop by the gift shop at the cave, which sells handcrafted items made by local artisans. These include replicas of Taino art found in the cave.

Quick Travel Tips

Best Times to Visit: November to April for the best weather across the island.

Avoiding Crowds: Try to visit popular spots like Saona Island and El Limón Waterfall early in the morning or on weekdays.
Budget-Friendly Tip: Public transportation is affordable and reliable for getting between major cities, but private shuttles and taxis offer comfort and convenience for short trips.

Each destination in the Dominican Republic has its personality, offering something different to every traveler. From historical landmarks to natural wonders, there's always something to see, and with nearby attractions and hidden gems, your trip can be full of surprises. With this guide, you'll be well-prepared to enjoy every corner of this beautiful island.

➢Beaches in the Dominican Republic

The beaches of the Dominican Republic are nothing short of spectacular. With over 800 miles of coastline, this island offers everything from lively, resort-lined shores to secluded coves perfect for a quiet escape. Whether you're soaking up the sun on the famous beaches of Punta Cana or discovering hidden gems along the Samaná Peninsula, each beach has its charm.

The warm, clear waters are ideal for swimming, snorkeling, and a variety of water sports. Beyond the natural beauty, these beaches offer a blend of local culture, relaxation, and adventure that keeps visitors coming back year after year. Here is a guide to the top beaches according to the top destinations we've covered earlier that you shouldn't miss while in the Dominican Republic.

1. Santo Domingo and Surrounding Areas

While Santo Domingo is best known for its colonial history, the nearby beaches provide excellent opportunities for relaxation and water activities. Here are three top beaches near the capital:

- **Playa Najayo**

Dominican Republic Travel Guide 2025

Overview:

Located just an hour west of Santo Domingo, Playa Najayo offers a mix of golden sand and rocky outcrops, making it a favorite among locals. The calm waters are perfect for swimming, and the beachside restaurants serve fresh seafood, making this an ideal spot for a laid-back beach day close to the city.

SCAN TO ACCESS
PLAYA NAJAYO

Dominican Republic Travel Guide 2025

What Makes It Special:

Local Atmosphere: This beach is mostly frequented by locals, giving it an authentic Dominican vibe.

Fresh Seafood: Enjoy freshly caught fish at one of the small beachside huts.

Less Crowded: Despite being close to Santo Domingo, Playa Najayo remains relatively uncrowded compared to more popular tourist destinations.

Local Tips:

Best Time to Visit: Weekdays are quieter, as weekends tend to attract more local families.

How to Get There: From Santo Domingo, take the highway west toward San Cristóbal. Public buses ("guaguas") also run along this route, costing around $3.

- **Playa Palenque**

Dominican Republic Travel Guide 2025

Overview:

About 40 minutes from Santo Domingo, Playa Palenque is a small yet charming beach known for its relaxed vibe and crystal-clear waters. The beach is lined with palms, creating natural shaded areas for a perfect afternoon escape from the bustling city.

SCAN TO ACCESS PLAYA PALENQUE

What Makes It Special:

Dominican Republic Travel Guide 2025

Serene Waters: The shallow, calm waters make it great for families with small children.

Local Vendors: You'll find a variety of street vendors selling fried fish, tostones (fried plantains), and coconut water.

Local Tips:

Nearby Attractions: Combine a visit to Playa Palenque with a stop at Salto de Palenque, a beautiful nearby waterfall.

How to Get There: It's a quick 40-minute drive from Santo Domingo via Autopista 6 de Noviembre. Alternatively, take a bus from the Parque Enriquillo bus terminal in Santo Domingo for about $3.

- **Playa Guayacanes**

Overview: Playa Guayacanes, located just east of Santo Domingo, is a picturesque fishing village turned beach haven. With its turquoise waters, soft white sand, and palm trees swaying in the breeze, it's a peaceful alternative to the more tourist-heavy beaches of the Dominican Republic.

Dominican Republic Travel Guide 2025

What Makes It Special:

Fishing Village Charm: Watch local fishermen haul in their catch in the mornings, a tradition that adds to the authentic Dominican experience.

Quiet and Peaceful: This beach is more relaxed compared to nearby Boca Chica, making it perfect for unwinding.

Local Tips:

Best Time to Visit: Early mornings provide a peaceful atmosphere, while the afternoons bring more beachgoers from nearby towns.

How to Get There: It's a 45-minute drive east from Santo Domingo along the Autopista Las Américas. Public buses are also available, costing around $2.

2. **Puerto Plata and the North Coast**

Dominican Republic Travel Guide 2025

Known for its diverse coastal landscape, Puerto Plata offers some of the best beaches on the north coast of the Dominican Republic.

- **Playa Encuentro**

Overview: Just outside the town of Cabarete, Playa Encuentro is a hidden gem for surfers and adventurers. This beach is renowned for its consistent waves and surf schools, making it a go-to destination for both beginner and experienced surfers.

SCAN TO ACCESS PLAYA ENCUENTRO

What Makes It Special:

Surfing Paradise: Encuentro is one of the best surf spots in the Caribbean, with waves perfect for all skill levels.

Authentic Vibe: The beach is quiet, lined with small surf shops and cafes, providing a laid-back, bohemian atmosphere.

Dominican Republic Travel Guide 2025

Local Tips:

Surf Lessons: Book a lesson with one of the local surf schools for around $35-50 USD per session.

How to Get There: From Puerto Plata, drive east toward Cabarete. Playa Encuentro is about a 25-minute drive. You can also take a local "guagua" bus for $1 from Cabarete.

- **Playa Cabarete**

Overview: Known as the kiteboarding and windsurfing capital of the Dominican Republic, Playa Cabarete is a lively, bustling beach with plenty of action on the water. The golden sands and steady winds make it a favorite for water sports enthusiasts.

SCAN TO ACCESS PLAYA CABARETE

What Makes It Special:

Dominican Republic Travel Guide 2025

Kiteboarding Hub: The steady winds year-round attract kiteboarders from all over the world.

Nightlife: After a day on the water, enjoy Cabarete's lively beach bars and restaurants.

Local Tips:

Kiteboarding Rentals: Lessons and rentals are available for around $70-100 USD for a two-hour session.

How to Get There: From Puerto Plata, drive east along the Ruta 5 to Cabarete (30 minutes). Public transport via "guagua" buses also runs regularly for about $1-2 USD.

- **Playa Costambar**

Overview: Playa Costambar is a peaceful alternative to Puerto Plata's more touristy beaches, offering a laid-back experience with a mix of locals and expats. This beach is perfect for a quiet day by the water, with calm waves and fewer vendors.

Dominican Republic Travel Guide 2025

SCAN TO ACCESS PLAYA COSTAMBAR

What Makes It Special:

Relaxed Vibe: Costambar is less commercialized than Playa Dorada, offering a more tranquil and local atmosphere.

Calm Waters: Ideal for swimming and families, with shallow, warm waters.

Local Tips:

Sunset Views: Stick around for the sunset; Playa Costambar offers one of the best spots to watch the sun dip into the ocean.

How to Get There: It's a 10-minute drive from Puerto Plata. There is limited public transportation, so taking a taxi or rental car is recommended.

3. Samaná Peninsula

A haven for eco-tourism and natural beauty, Samaná offers some of the most remote and pristine beaches in the Dominican Republic.

- **Playa Las Galeras**

Overview: Located at the eastern tip of the Samaná Peninsula, Playa Las Galeras is a tranquil beach known for its crystal-clear waters and scenic views of nearby islands. This remote paradise is perfect for those looking to escape the hustle and bustle of busier tourist areas.

SCAN TO ACCESS PLAYA LAS GALERAS

What Makes It Special:

Secluded Beauty: With fewer tourists, this beach feels like a hidden paradise.

Dominican Republic Travel Guide 2025

Spectacular Views: Stunning vistas of Cabo Cabrón and Cabo Samaná from the beach.

Local Tips:

Best Time to Visit: Early mornings offer the most peaceful atmosphere before locals and visitors arrive.

How to Get There: From Samaná town, take a bus or taxi to Las Galeras (around 45 minutes, $5-10 USD).

- **Playa Cayo Levantado**

Overview: Also known as Bacardi Island, Playa Cayo Levantado offers an idyllic island escape just off the coast of Samaná Bay. With its postcard-perfect scenery, this beach is ideal for a day trip from the mainland.

SCAN TO ACCESS
PLAYA CAYO
LEVANTADO

What Makes It Special:

Dominican Republic Travel Guide 2025

Island Paradise: A small, stunning island beach with soft sand and clear waters.

Famous Rum Spot: The island is nicknamed Bacardi Island due to its resemblance to a popular Bacardi rum ad.

Local Tips:

Getting There: Boats depart regularly from the Samaná Pier. Round-trip boat fare is around $10-20 USD.

What to Bring: The island offers beach bars and restaurants, but it's advisable to bring your snacks and drinks if you prefer a quieter experience.

Dominican Republic Travel Guide 2025

CHAPTER 5: WHERE TO STAY

Finding the perfect place to stay can make or break your trip, and the Dominican Republic offers no shortage of options. Whether you're looking for a luxury resort with all the bells and whistles, a cozy mid-range hotel with local charm, or a budget-friendly spot near the beach, there's something here for every traveler.

In this chapter, we'll help you navigate the best accommodations across the island, from beachfront escapes to city stays, ensuring you have a comfortable and memorable trip—no matter your budget.

➢Luxury Hotels

For travelers looking for the best that the Dominican Republic has to offer, the luxury hotels on this list provide exceptional comfort, world-class amenities, and unique experiences that make for an unforgettable stay.

- **Tortuga Bay Hotel at Puntacana Resort (Punta Cana)**

Tortuga Bay Hotel sets the standard for luxury in Punta Cana, with suites designed by the late Oscar de la Renta and an emphasis on sustainability. Guests enjoy private beach access, top-tier spa services, and gourmet dining options.

SCAN TO ACCESS TORTUGA BAY HOTEL AT PUNTACANA RESORT (PUNTA CANA)

Why It Stands Out: Eco-conscious luxury, beachfront villas, exclusive airport transfers.

Location: Punta Cana Resort & Golf Club, Higüey 23000, Dominican Republic

Contact Info: +1 809-959-8229

Dominican Republic Travel Guide 2025

Pro Tip: Book a beachfront villa for direct ocean views and VIP service at the resort.

- **Amanera (Playa Grande)**

Amanera offers a secluded, peaceful retreat with breathtaking views of the Atlantic Ocean. Its minimalist design is a perfect match for those who want to relax in privacy while enjoying one of the most scenic golf courses in the Caribbean.

SCAN TO ACCESS AMANERA (PLAYA GRANDE)

Why It Stands Out: Stunning views, private pools, a world-class golf course, and direct beach access.

Location: Auto. 5. Carretera, Carretera, Rio San Juan 33300, Dominican Republic

Contact Info: +1 809-589-2888

Dominican Republic Travel Guide 2025

Pro Tip: Try the beachside massage to truly unwind with the sound of the waves.

- **Eden Roc Cap Cana (Punta Cana)**

Set within the exclusive Cap Cana community, Eden Roc blends Mediterranean elegance with Caribbean warmth. The private suites and bungalows, some with personal pools, offer high-end luxury with all the privacy you could want.

SCAN TO ACCESS EDEN ROC CAP CANA (PUNTA CANA)

Why It Stands Out: Private beach, marina access, golf course, and world-class dining.

Location: Cap Cana, Punta Cana, Provincia La Altagracia, Punta Cana 23000, Dominican Republic

Contact Info: +1 809-469-7469

Pro Tip: For honeymooners, the beachfront bungalows offer the best of privacy and romance.

Dominican Republic Travel Guide 2025

- **Casa Colonial Beach & Spa (Puerto Plata)**

Casa Colonial combines colonial charm with modern luxury on the shores of Playa Dorada. This boutique hotel is perfect for travelers who want a more intimate experience without sacrificing luxury.

SCAN TO ACCESS CASA COLONIAL BEACH & SPA (PUERTO PLATA)

Why It Stands Out: Rooftop infinity pool, award-winning Bagua Spa, beachfront views.

Location: Puerto Plata 57000, Dominican Republic

Contact Info: +1 809-320-3232

Pro Tip: Enjoy sunset cocktails on the rooftop pool deck—it's the best seat in the house.

- **Zoëtry Agua Punta Cana**

Zoëtry offers an all-inclusive experience focused on wellness and tranquility. With organic food, daily wellness activities, and an emphasis on relaxation, it's an ideal choice for those seeking a peaceful getaway.

SCAN TO ACCESS ZOËTRY AGUA PUNTA CANA

Why It Stands Out: Wellness-focused, daily yoga and meditation, organic dining options.

Location: Playas De, Punta Cana 23301, Dominican Republic

Contact Info: +1 809-468-0000.

Pro Tip: Take advantage of the complimentary wellness consultation to kick off a rejuvenating stay.

➤Mid-Range Hotels

If you're looking for value without sacrificing comfort, these mid-range hotels offer a balance of affordability and great amenities. Whether you're traveling as a family, a couple, or solo, these properties provide comfortable accommodations with plenty of perks.

- **Viva Wyndham V Samana (Las Terrenas)**

A stylish, adults-only, all-inclusive resort, Viva Wyndham offers excellent beach access, a full range of activities, and a laid-back atmosphere perfect for couples or friends.

SCAN TO ACCESS VIVA WYNDHAM V SAMANA (LAS TERRENAS)

Why It Stands Out: All-inclusive, yoga and water sports, beachfront rooms.

Location: 8C29+HW, Blvd. Turístico del Atlántico, Las Terrenas 32000, Dominican Republic

Contact Info: +1 809-240-6600

Pro Tip: Book one of the beachfront "Vibe Rooms" for direct access to the sand and a private plunge pool.

- **Bahia Principe Grand El Portillo (Las Terrenas)**

Perfect for families, Bahia Principe offers spacious suites, an easygoing atmosphere, and plenty of activities for kids and adults alike.

SCAN TO ACCESS BAHIA PRINCIPE GRAND EL PORTILLO (LAS TERRENAS)

Why It Stands Out: Family-friendly, kids' club, beach access, multiple dining options.

Location: Crta. Las Terrenas - El Limón, km. 4, Las Terrenas, Dominican Republic

Contact Info: +1 809-240-6100

Pro Tip: Make sure to explore the coral reefs just offshore—snorkeling gear is available for free at the hotel.

- **The Bannister Hotel & Yacht Club (Samaná)**

Dominican Republic Travel Guide 2025

For travelers seeking a bit of adventure with comfort, The Bannister Hotel offers a marina-side setting with views over Samaná Bay. A bit off the beaten path, it's great for those who want a mix of luxury and mid-range pricing.

SCAN TO ACCESS THE BANNISTER HOTEL & YACHT CLUB (SAMANÁ)

Why It Stands Out: Marina access, spacious suites, infinity pool.

Location: Calle María Trinidad Sánchez 5, Samaná 32000, Dominican Republic

Contact Info: +1 809-503-6363

Pro Tip: Book a boat tour through the marina for a day of whale watching during the winter months.

- **Emotions by Hodelpa (Juan Dolio)**

Just a short drive from Santo Domingo, this all-inclusive resort provides an affordable beachside stay with

Dominican Republic Travel Guide 2025

multiple pools, family-friendly amenities, and easy access to Juan Dolio's local restaurants and shops.

SCAN TO ACCESS EMOTIONS BY HODELPA (JUAN DOLIO)

Why It Stands Out: Family-friendly, beach access, multiple dining options, and pools.

Location: Juan De, Autovía del Este, Playa Juan Dolio 21004, Dominican Republic

Contact Info: +1 809-339-9555

Pro Tip: Explore the local dining scene in Juan Dolio—there are some great local spots just a short walk from the hotel.

- **BlueBay Villas Doradas (Puerto Plata)**

A laid-back, adults-only retreat, BlueBay offers a budget-friendly escape with all the perks of a higher-end resort. With easy access to Playa Dorada, it's a perfect spot for couples seeking a quiet, relaxing stay.

Dominican Republic Travel Guide 2025

```
SCAN TO ACCESS
BLUEBAY
VILLAS
DORADAS
(PUERTO PLATA)
```

Why It Stands Out Beach access, adults-only, spa services, and golf nearby.

Location: 538, Calle Principal Complejo Playa Dorada, Puerto Plata 57000, Dominican Republic

Contact Info: +1 809-320-3000

Pro Tip: The hotel's beachfront massage is a must for relaxing after a day in the sun.

➢ Budget-Friendly Hotels

For travelers who want to save on accommodation but still enjoy a comfortable stay, these budget-friendly hotels offer clean, welcoming rooms with convenient

Dominican Republic Travel Guide 2025

locations. You don't have to spend a fortune to enjoy the Dominican Republic.

- **Hostal La Colonia (Santo Domingo)**

Located in the historic Colonial Zone of Santo Domingo, this charming guesthouse offers travelers a budget-friendly option in the heart of the city's most vibrant area.

Why It Stands Out: Close to major historic sites, free Wi-Fi, and clean rooms.

Location: C. Isabel La Católica 110, Santo Domingo 10210, Dominican Republic

Contact Info: +1 829-532-7878

Pro Tip: Ask the staff for recommendations—they're great at pointing you to the best local dining spots.

Dominican Republic Travel Guide 2025

- **Hotel Villa Iguana (Bayahibe)**

Affordable Comfort Near the Beach

Hotel Villa Iguana is a budget-friendly option located in the heart of Bayahibe. The hotel offers clean, cozy rooms with a rooftop pool, and it's just a short walk from the beach and the town's restaurants and shops. Guests can easily access boat tours to Isla Saona and enjoy the relaxed atmosphere of this coastal village.

SCAN TO ACCESS HOTEL VILLA IGUANA (BAYAHIBE)

Key Amenities: Rooftop pool, free breakfast, tour assistance.

Location: C. Tomasa Cedeño 2, Bayahíbe 23000, Dominican Republic

Contact Info: +1 829-546-0400

Insider Tip: The rooftop is perfect for unwinding after a day at the beach, offering great sunset views.

Dominican Republic Travel Guide 2025

- **Hotel Zapata (Boca Chica)**

Located right on Boca Chica Beach, Hotel Zapata is a budget-friendly, no-frills option that's perfect for those who want to be close to the water without paying resort prices.

SCAN TO ACCESS HOTEL ZAPATA (BOCA CHICA)

Why It Stands Out: Beachfront access, affordable rates, airport shuttle service.

Location: Abraham Nunez 27, Boca Chica, Dominican Republic.

Contact Info: +1 809-523-4777

Pro Tip: Enjoy fresh seafood at the nearby local restaurants, where you can dine like a local for a fraction of the cost.

- **Sublime Samana Hotel & Residences**

Dominican Republic Travel Guide 2025

Luxurious Beachfront Escape

Sublime Samana is a boutique hotel that offers a perfect mix of luxury and nature. Located on a secluded beach just outside Las Terrenas, it provides spacious suites and villas with private terraces and access to a pristine stretch of sand. The hotel's amenities include a spa, gourmet restaurant, and two pools, making it ideal for those looking for relaxation and exclusivity.

SCAN TO ACCESS SUBLIME SAMANA HOTEL & RESIDENCES

Key Amenities: Beachfront access, spa, gourmet dining, two pools, private villas.

Location: 7CW2+MH4 Playa Coson, Las Terrenas 32000, Dominican Republic

Contact Info: +1 809-240-5050

Insider Tip: Book a beachfront villa for a private outdoor shower and stunning views of the ocean.

Dominican Republic Travel Guide 2025

- **Cabarete Palm Beach Condos**

Located right on Cabarete Beach, Cabarete Palm Beach Condos is an excellent option for travelers seeking affordable, self-catering accommodation. With condos offering kitchen facilities and balconies overlooking the ocean, it's ideal for those wanting to enjoy kiteboarding and windsurfing just steps from their door.

SCAN TO ACCESS CABARETE PALM BEACH CONDOS

Key Amenities: Beachfront access, pool, full kitchens in condos, free Wi-Fi.

Location: Cabarete 57000, Dominican Republic

Contact Info: +1 809-571-0758

Insider Tip: Book a condo with a balcony for incredible ocean views, especially at sunrise.

Dominican Republic Travel Guide 2025

The Dominican Republic offers a wide range of accommodation options to suit every traveler's taste and budget. For those seeking luxury, Punta Cana is renowned for its all-inclusive resorts, where palm-lined beaches meet five-star amenities, perfect for indulgent relaxation. If you're looking for a more laid-back experience, the Samaná Peninsula is a haven for eco-conscious travelers, with charming boutique hotels and eco-lodges tucked away in lush, tropical landscapes.

In Santo Domingo, history lovers can stay in beautifully restored colonial-era hotels within the Zona Colonial, steps away from UNESCO-listed landmarks and vibrant cafes. Puerto Plata blends adventure with comfort, offering beachfront resorts that are ideal for exploring nearby attractions like the 27 Waterfalls or the famed cable car ride to Mount Isabel de Torres.

For those on a budget, areas like Las Terrenas in Samaná or Jarabacoa in the mountains provide affordable yet memorable stays, with guesthouses and small hotels offering warm Dominican hospitality. Whether you're after a lavish beach escape or a serene retreat into nature, the Dominican Republic has a place to rest your head after a day of adventure.

Booking Accommodations During Peak and Off-Peak Seasons

Peak season (December to April): Hotels and resorts are often fully booked, so it is essential to reserve accommodations 3-6 months in advance.

Off-peak season (May to November): Prices are lower, and last-minute bookings are possible. However, travelers should note that hurricane season runs from June to November, which may affect availability and prices.

Reliable booking platforms:

- **Booking.com:** Excellent for a range of accommodation types, from luxury resorts to budget hotels.
- **Airbnb:** Offers unique stays, including eco-lodges and vacation rentals.
- **Expedia:** Good for booking all-inclusive resorts and package deals.

- **Hotels.com:** Offers competitive prices and reward points for frequent bookings.
- **Travelocity:** Ideal for deals on flights and accommodation bundles.

★Tips for Booking Accommodations

- **Book Early for Popular Spots**

The Dominican Republic is a year-round destination, but high season (December to April) can see accommodations fill up fast, especially in Punta Cana and Santo Domingo. Booking several months in advance ensures the best rates and availability.

- **Consider All-Inclusive Resorts**

For travelers seeking convenience, many resorts offer all-inclusive packages that cover meals, drinks, and activities. This can be a good value, particularly in beach areas like Punta Cana or La Romana. Be sure to read reviews to assess the quality of food and services.

- **Stay Flexible with Location**

Dominican Republic Travel Guide 2025

For more affordable stays, look beyond the main tourist hubs. Towns like Bayahibe or Cabarete offer charming alternatives, often with lower prices and fewer crowds, while still providing easy access to beaches and local attractions.

- **Look for Sustainable and Eco-Friendly Options**

The Dominican Republic is home to a growing number of eco-lodges and green-certified hotels. If sustainability is important to you, seek out properties that prioritize environmental conservation, especially around the Samaná Peninsula and Jarabacoa.

- **Check Amenities and Reviews Carefully**

Amenities can vary widely between accommodations. If air conditioning, Wi-Fi, or included breakfast are must-haves, make sure to check the fine print and read recent guest reviews for up-to-date insights on cleanliness and service.

Dominican Republic Travel Guide 2025

CHAPTER 6: NATURE AND OUTDOOR ADVENTURES

The Dominican Republic is often celebrated for its pristine beaches, but it's the rugged, untouched beauty of the country's national parks and nature reserves that captivates adventurous souls. From lush rainforests teeming with exotic wildlife to the towering heights of Pico Duarte, the highest peak in the Caribbean, the Dominican Republic offers a paradise for nature lovers and outdoor enthusiasts alike. Whether you're hiking through mist-covered mountains, paddling along quiet rivers, or spotting rare birds in remote jungles, this island promises unforgettable outdoor experiences.

- **Los Haitises National Park: A Haven for Nature Lovers**

Dominican Republic Travel Guide 2025

Los Haitises National Park

Located on the Samaná Bay, Los Haitises National Park is a protected wonderland of mangroves, limestone caves, and ancient Taino petroglyphs. This park is a dream for birdwatchers, with more than 200 species calling it home, including pelicans, herons, and the endangered Ridgway's Hawk. Explore the park by boat, weaving through lush islets and mangrove canals, and visit the impressive caves like Cueva de la Arena, where Taino rock art can still be seen.

Dominican Republic Travel Guide 2025

SCAN TO ACCESS
LOS HAITISES
NATIONAL PARK

How to Access:

Boat Tour: Most visitors reach Los Haitises via boat tours from Samaná or Sabana de la Mar. Tours generally cost around $50 USD and can be arranged through local operators like Whale Samaná.

Getting There:

From Samaná, it's a scenic 30-minute boat ride to the park. Travelers from Santo Domingo can take a 2-hour drive to Sabana de la Mar, followed by a short boat transfer.

Local Tip: Bring binoculars for birdwatching and eco-friendly sunscreen to protect the park's fragile ecosystem.

Dominican Republic Travel Guide 2025

- **Pico Duarte: Conquer the Caribbean's Highest Peak**

At 3,087 meters (10,128 feet), Pico Duarte is the highest mountain in the Caribbean and a must for serious hikers. The trek to the summit is challenging but rewarding, offering breathtaking views over mountain ranges and cloud forests. The most popular route starts from the town of La Ciénaga, and the journey typically takes two to three days, depending on fitness level and weather conditions.

SCAN TO ACCESS PICO DUARTE

Hiking Route Overview:

Distance: The round-trip hike from La Ciénaga covers 46 kilometers (28 miles).

Difficulty Level: Moderate to difficult, requiring good physical fitness.

Dominican Republic Travel Guide 2025

Necessary Equipment: Sturdy hiking boots, warm clothing (it can get cold at the summit), and plenty of water. It's also highly recommended to hike with a guide, which can be arranged in Jarabacoa for around $80-100 USD per person.

Local Guide: Contact Rancho Baiguate in Jarabacoa for guided tours and mule support for carrying gear. They offer comprehensive packages that include meals, camping gear, and park entrance fees.

Eco-Tourism and River Adventures in Jarabacoa

Known as the adventure capital of the Dominican Republic, Jarabacoa offers an abundance of eco-tourism activities. Surrounded by waterfalls, rivers, and lush valleys, this mountain town is the perfect base for thrill-seekers.

River Rafting: Tackle the rapids of the Yaque del Norte, the longest river in the Caribbean. Rafting tours, which cost around $60 USD, are available through local operators like Jarabacoa River Club, and they cater to both beginners and experienced rafters.

Dominican Republic Travel Guide 2025

Birdwatching: The forests around Jarabacoa are home to rare species like the Hispaniolan Trogon. Opt for a guided birdwatching hike early in the morning for the best chances of spotting native species.

Canyoning and Waterfall Rappelling: For a more adrenaline-fueled experience, try canyoning at Salto de Jimenoa, one of the area's most beautiful waterfalls.
Getting There:

From Santo Domingo: A 2-hour drive by car or a 3-hour bus ride to Jarabacoa.
From Santiago: It's a scenic 1-hour drive by car or bus. Once in Jarabacoa, most eco-tours can be arranged through local agencies or your hotel.

Local Tip: For a unique experience, book a stay in an eco-lodge like Rancho Baiguate, which focuses on sustainable tourism and offers direct access to many outdoor activities.

Supporting Eco-Friendly Travel

Dominican Republic Travel Guide 2025

Travelers to the Dominican Republic can support conservation efforts by choosing eco-friendly tours and accommodations that prioritize sustainability. Many parks and reserves are fragile ecosystems, so it's crucial to practice responsible tourism:

- **Leave No Trace**: When hiking or exploring natural areas, always take your trash with you. Avoid disturbing wildlife and stay on marked trails to protect plant life.
- **Use Eco-Friendly Products:** Pack biodegradable toiletries, reef-safe sunscreen, and reusable water bottles. By avoiding plastic waste, you help preserve the island's pristine landscapes.
- **Support Local Communities**: Book tours and stay in accommodations that give back to the local community. Many eco-lodges and local operators reinvest profits into environmental conservation and community development.

Local Tip: Stay at Eco-Lodge Taino in Samaná, where solar power and organic farming practices are in place, and a portion of your stay directly supports reforestation efforts.

The Dominican Republic is a land of diverse natural beauty, from towering peaks to hidden caves, from serene rivers to rich rainforests alive with the sounds of birds. Whether you're scaling Pico Duarte or drifting through Los Haitises' mangroves, the island offers adventures that connect you deeply to the environment. By supporting eco-tourism and making mindful travel choices, you're not just enjoying these treasures—you're helping to preserve them for generations to come.

So lace up your boots, grab your binoculars, and prepare to experience the wild, untamed side of the Dominican Republic—where nature and adventure go hand in hand, and every step leads to discovery.

Cultural Experiences in the Dominican Republic

Dominican Republic Travel Guide 2025

The Dominican Republic's rich cultural heritage is an essential part of its identity, and for those eager to dive deeper into its history and traditions, there's no shortage of vibrant museums, historic landmarks, and lively festivals to explore.

From ancient colonial architecture to the rhythm of merengue in the streets, the cultural heartbeat of the island is palpable at every turn.

➢Museums and Historic Sites

- **Museo de las Casas Reales**

One of the most significant museums in the Zona Colonial, the Museo de las Casas Reales offers a fascinating glimpse into the colonial history of the Dominican Republic. Housed in a stunning 16th-century building, this museum was originally the seat of the Spanish Crown's administrative offices in the New World. The exhibits focus on the early governance, culture, and military life of the island during the Spanish colonial period.

Dominican Republic Travel Guide 2025

SCAN TO ACCESS MUSEO DE LAS CASAS REALES

Getting There:

Located in the heart of the Zona Colonial, it's a short 10-minute walk from most nearby hotels, or a 5-minute taxi ride from the Malecón.

Location: C. Las Damas, Santo Domingo 10210, Dominican Republic

Contact Info: +1 809-682-4202

Entry Cost:

$3 USD for adults, free for children under 10.

Best Time to Visit:

Mornings are best for fewer crowds and cooler temperatures, especially if you plan to explore other nearby historic sites.

- **Fortaleza Ozama (Santo Domingo)**

Dominican Republic Travel Guide 2025

This stone fortress, built in the early 1500s, is the oldest in the Americas and played a key role in protecting Santo Domingo from pirate attacks. Visitors can tour the tower, dungeons, and grounds, all while enjoying sweeping views of the Ozama River.

SCAN TO ACCESS FORTALEZA OZAMA

Getting There:

Dominican Republic Travel Guide 2025

The fortress is located along the Calle Las Damas, just a short walk from Alcázar de Colón, making it easy to visit both in one day.

Location: C. Las Damas 1, Santo Domingo 10210, Dominican Republic

Contact Info: +1 809-688-1553

Entry Cost:
$2 USD.

Best Time to Visit:
Late afternoon offers cooler temperatures and dramatic views of the setting sun over the river.

- **Panteón Nacional (Santo Domingo)**

Located on Calle Las Damas, the Panteón Nacional is a former Jesuit church that has been transformed into a national monument, honoring the Dominican Republic's heroes. The impressive architecture and solemn atmosphere make it a must-see for history buffs. Inside, an eternal flame burns in memory of the country's most honored figures.

Dominican Republic Travel Guide 2025

```
SCAN TO ACCESS
   PANTEÓN
   NACIONAL
```

Getting There:

The Panteón Nacional is just a 10-minute walk from most locations within the Zona Colonial.

Location: F4G8+2M9, C. Las Damas, Santo Domingo 10210, Dominican Republic

Entry Cost:

Free.

Best Time to Visit:

Visit in the early afternoon to experience the quiet solemnity of the monument, and to take in the architectural beauty of this historic building.

- **Museo del Hombre Dominicano (Santo Domingo)**

Dominican Republic Travel Guide 2025

For those interested in the indigenous cultures of the island, the Museo del Hombre Dominicano is a must-visit. The museum houses artifacts from the Taíno civilization, the first inhabitants of the island, along with displays about the island's African and Spanish cultural influences. From ancient pottery to ceremonial objects, this museum offers a comprehensive look at the rich, diverse history of the Dominican Republic.

SCAN TO ACCESS MUSEO DEL HOMBRE DOMINICANO

Getting There:
Located in Plaza de la Cultura, it's a 10-minute taxi ride from the Zona Colonial or a short walk from Teatro Nacional.
Location: Plaza de la Cultura Juan Pablo Duarte, Av. Pedro Henríquez Ureña, Santo Domingo 10204, Dominican Republic
Contact Info: +1 809-687-3622

Dominican Republic Travel Guide 2025

Entry Cost:

$4 USD for adults.

Best Time to Visit:

Weekdays are ideal, with fewer crowds and plenty of time to explore the in-depth exhibits at your own pace.

CHAPTER 7: FESTIVALS AND EVENTS

The Dominican Republic comes alive with music, dance, and color during its many festivals, each celebrating a unique aspect of its cultural heritage.

- **Carnival (February)**

Celebrated throughout the country, Carnival is a vibrant, month-long event culminating in wild parades filled with music, dancers in elaborate costumes, and lively street parties. The biggest and most famous celebrations take place in Santo Domingo and La Vega.

How to Participate:
Tourists are encouraged to join the festivities by dressing in colorful costumes or face masks, a nod to the event's African and Taíno influences. Be sure to book

Dominican Republic Travel Guide 2025

accommodation early, especially in La Vega, where the Carnival parades are legendary.

Local Tip:

For a more authentic experience, venture to smaller towns where local traditions shine. For example, Puerto Plata's Carnival offers a more intimate atmosphere with fewer tourists.

- **Merengue Festival (July/August)**

Merengue is the heartbeat of the Dominican Republic, and this festival honors the genre with days of non-stop music, dancing, and performances. The largest celebration takes place in Santo Domingo along the Malecón, where stages are set up for live bands and dance competitions.

How to Participate:

Admission is free, and the festival is open to all. Simply follow the sound of the music and join in. If you're new to merengue, don't worry—locals will be more than happy to show you the steps!

Local Tip:

Dominican Republic Travel Guide 2025

Arrive early to grab a spot near the main stage, or venture further down the Malecón to find smaller dance areas where spontaneous street performances break out.

➤Markets for Traditional Crafts

For a true taste of Dominican artistry, head to local markets where you'll find handcrafted jewelry, ceramics, and traditional wooden sculptures.

- **Mercado Modelo (Santo Domingo)**

Located in the heart of the city, this sprawling market is known for its vibrant atmosphere and endless rows of vendors selling everything from larimar jewelry (a blue gemstone unique to the Dominican Republic) to handwoven baskets and colorful paintings.

SCAN TO ACCESS MERCADO MODELO

Dominican Republic Travel Guide 2025

How to Avoid Overpriced Items:

Always bargain respectfully. Most items are priced with negotiation in mind, so offering about 50-60% of the initial price is a good starting point. Also, shop around and compare prices between stalls before making a purchase.

Local Tip:

If you're looking for high-quality larimar or amber jewelry, ask vendors for certification to ensure authenticity.

- **Altos de Chavón Artisan Village (La Romana)**

Set within the charming Altos de Chavón, a replica of a 16th-century Mediterranean village, this artisan market is a must-visit for those looking to explore both culture and craftsmanship. Local artisans sell handmade pottery, jewelry, and paintings in quaint stone cottages lining the cobblestone streets. The village itself is a cultural attraction, with working artists in residence, galleries, and craft workshops.

Dominican Republic Travel Guide 2025

SCAN TO ACCESS ALTOS DE CHAVÓN

Getting There:

Located within Casa de Campo Resort in La Romana, it's about a 15-minute drive from central La Romana. If you're staying at the resort, shuttles are available, or you can take a taxi for about $15 USD.

Local Tip:

Spend extra time exploring the village itself—there's an art school, amphitheater, and stunning views of the Chavón River. For souvenirs, look for pottery and wood carvings made by local artisans.

➢Live Music and Dance Performances

Merengue and bachata are the soul of Dominican music, and there's no shortage of venues where you can experience live performances.

- **Jet Set Club**

A legendary venue in Santo Domingo, Jet Set Club is where you'll find some of the best live performances of merengue, bachata, and salsa. This club has hosted renowned Dominican artists and international stars, offering an energetic and authentic music scene. Locals and visitors alike flock here on Monday nights for live concerts that often feature top acts in Dominican music. The vibrant atmosphere and dance floor make it a must-visit for anyone wanting to experience the true rhythm of the Dominican Republic.

Dominican Republic Travel Guide 2025

SCAN TO ACCESS JET SET CLUB

Getting There:

Located just outside the city center in Avenida Independencia, it's about a 15-minute taxi ride from the Zona Colonial, costing around $10-15 USD.

Local Tip:

Arrive early (before 10 PM) to grab a good spot near the stage. Dress to impress, as locals often come dressed up for a night of dancing and live music.

- **Casa de Teatro (Santo Domingo)**

Located in the Zona Colonial, Casa de Teatro is a cultural hub featuring live music, theater, and art exhibitions. It's the perfect spot to catch intimate merengue or jazz performances, often accompanied by local dancers. The venue also serves as a gathering place for local artists, making it a great spot to immerse yourself in the city's creative scene.

SCAN TO ACCESS CASA DE TEATRO

Local Tip:
Check the event schedule ahead of time for special performances or themed nights. Performances usually start around 9 PM, and there's a cozy bar where you can enjoy a drink while soaking in the atmosphere.

- **Jalao (Santo Domingo)**

For a combination of live music and Dominican cuisine, Jalao in the heart of the Zona Colonial offers a unique experience. This lively restaurant-bar regularly hosts live performances of merengue, bachata, and salsa, all while serving delicious traditional Dominican dishes. The vibrant decor and central location make it a perfect spot for both dinner and a night of dancing. As the night progresses, the music picks up, and the crowd spills onto the dance floor, making it a great way to experience the local music scene in a more intimate setting.

SCAN TO ACCESS JALAO

Getting There:
Jalao is conveniently located on Calle El Conde, right in the Zona Colonial, making it a short walk from most nearby hotels.

Local Tip:
Make a reservation for dinner before the show and stay for the music and dancing afterward. The lively atmosphere makes it a favorite for both locals and tourists, so it can get busy on weekends.

Dominican Republic Travel Guide 2025

The Dominican Republic is a treasure trove of cultural experiences, blending its rich history with vibrant modern-day traditions. Whether you're wandering the halls of colonial-era fortresses, joining in the rhythmic celebration of a merengue festival, or shopping for hand-crafted treasures in a local market, the island invites you to not just observe its culture, but to live it. As you explore, take time to dance, discover, and connect with the Dominican spirit—it's an experience that will leave you enriched long after the music fades.

CHAPTER 8: FOOD AND DINING

Dominican cuisine is a vibrant fusion of Taíno, African, and Spanish influences, offering a rich tapestry of flavors that reflect the island's history and cultural diversity. Whether you're savoring hearty stews, indulging in tropical fruits, or trying out freshly caught seafood, Dominican food captures the essence of the island's laid-back yet flavorful lifestyle. For those visiting for the first time, sampling the local cuisine is not just about nourishment—it's a gateway to understanding the Dominican Republic's culinary soul.

➢Dishes to Try First

1. Sancocho

Often referred to as the national dish, Sancocho is a rich, slow-cooked stew traditionally made with a mix of meats (often chicken, beef, and pork), yucca, plantains, and root vegetables. It's a comfort food that Dominicans often enjoy during family gatherings or special occasions. Each spoonful feels like a warm embrace, and it's best accompanied by a side of white rice and avocado.

2. Mangu

A Dominican breakfast staple, Mangu is made from boiled and mashed green plantains, often topped with sautéed red onions. It's typically served with a side of "Los Tres Golpes"—fried cheese, salami, and eggs—making it a hearty way to start the day. You'll find mangu in most local eateries, especially in Santo Domingo's breakfast spots.

3. Tostones

For a quick snack, try Tostones—twice-fried green plantains that are crispy on the outside and soft on the inside. They're often served as a side dish or appetizer, accompanied by garlic dipping sauce or a spicy mayo.

4. Pescado Frito (Fried Fish)

Along the coasts, especially in regions like Punta Cana and Samaná, you'll encounter Pescado Frito, a freshly caught fish fried to perfection. Served with lime, fried plantains, and a cold Presidente beer, this dish is best enjoyed beachside.

5. Dulce de Coco

For dessert, try Dulce de Coco, a sweet treat made from coconut milk, sugar, and cinnamon. It's the perfect way to end a meal, especially for coconut lovers.

➢Where to Experience Authentic Dominican Food

1. Santo Domingo

As the capital city, Santo Domingo is filled with restaurants where you can experience authentic Dominican cuisine, from street food stalls to upscale eateries.

- **El Conuco:**

Dominican Republic Travel Guide 2025

For a true taste of Dominican tradition, head to El Conuco in the heart of the city. Known for its folkloric ambiance and live merengue performances, this restaurant serves classic dishes like Sancocho, Mofongo (mashed plantains with pork or seafood), and a variety of grilled meats.

SCAN TO ACCESS EL CONUCO

Address: C. Casimiro de Moya #152, Santo Domingo, Dominican Republic

Contact Info: +1 809-686-0129

Local Tip: Ask for a table on the terrace for a breezy, relaxing atmosphere.

- **Adrián Tropical:**

This popular restaurant has several locations across Santo Domingo and is a favorite among locals for both

Dominican Republic Travel Guide 2025

its food and sea views. Try their famous Sancocho or Chicharrón de Pollo (fried chicken) while watching the sunset over the Malecón.

SCAN TO ACCESS ADRIÁN TROPICAL

Address: Av. George Washington 1, Santo Domingo 10205, Dominican Republic.

Contact Info: +1 809-565-9236

Local Tip: The portions are large, so consider sharing if you want to save room for dessert.

2. Punta Cana

While Punta Cana is known for its all-inclusive resorts, there are still plenty of local restaurants where you can get a taste of authentic Dominican flavors outside the hotel dining halls.

Dominican Republic Travel Guide 2025

- **La Yola:**

Overlooking the marina in Puntacana Resort & Club, La Yola offers a fresh take on traditional Dominican seafood dishes. The restaurant is known for its Pescado Frito and grilled lobster, which are as fresh as they come.

SCAN TO ACCESS LA YOLA

Address: Punta Cana 23000, Dominican Republic.

Contact Info: +1 809-959-1010

Local Tip: Dine at sunset for a stunning view of the water.

- **Don Pio Restaurante:**

Located in the Bávaro area, this charming eatery offers authentic Dominican home cooking. Mangu, Mofongo, and a variety of fresh seafood dishes are highlights on the menu, making it a local favorite.

Dominican Republic Travel Guide 2025

SCAN TO ACCESS
DON PIO
RESTAURANTE

Address: Plaza Turquesa, Av. Alemania, Punta Cana 23000, Dominican Republic

Contact Info: +1 809-455-7373

Local Tip: Go for lunch and try their daily specials—it's where many locals gather for a quick and delicious meal.

➢ Must-Visit Food Markets

Food markets are the heart of Dominican food culture, offering fresh ingredients and unique local products that are integral to the country's cuisine.

- **Mercado Municipal (Higüey)**

For an authentic, local experience, head to the Mercado Municipal in Higüey. This bustling market is a hub of activity where you can find fresh produce, meats, seafood, and traditional Dominican goods. It's an excellent place to shop for local fruits, vegetables, and unique items like handmade cheeses and spices. Along with fresh food, you'll find vendors selling local crafts, making it a blend of culture and culinary discovery.

SCAN TO ACCESS MERCADO MUNICIPAL

Getting There:

Higüey is located about 30 minutes from Punta Cana. Taxis cost around $20-25 USD, or you can take a local bus for a cheaper option at about $3-4 USD.

Location: Las Carreras, Higüey 23000, Dominican Republic.

Local Tip:

Arrive early in the morning when the market is most lively, and don't hesitate to bargain for the best deals on

Dominican Republic Travel Guide 2025

local goods. Be sure to try the fresh tropical fruits like mangoes and passion fruit.

- **Mercado de la Pulga (Santo Domingo)**

For a unique twist on a traditional market, Mercado de la Pulga is Santo Domingo's bustling flea market, where you can find everything from fresh food to second-hand goods and antiques. While not your typical food market, it offers an incredible array of local products, including tropical fruits, vegetables, and locally grown herbs and spices. It's a colorful, chaotic market that gives visitors a taste of everyday life in the city.

SCAN TO ACCESS MERCADO DE LA PULGA

Getting There:

Dominican Republic Travel Guide 2025

Located on the outskirts of Santo Domingo, it's best reached by taxi or Uber, which costs around $10-12 USD from the Zona Colonial.

Location: HX7F+XWX, Carr. Merca Santo Domingo, Santo Domingo, Dominican Republic

Contact Info: +1 829-851-9415

Local Tip:

Visit in the early afternoon when the market is in full swing, and keep an eye out for small vendors selling local specialties like queso de hoja (Dominican string cheese) and freshly pressed sugarcane juice.

★Dining Etiquette and Tipping in the Dominican Republic

Dominican dining culture is warm and communal, and sharing food is a big part of everyday life. When dining at a local restaurant or cafe, it's customary to greet the staff with a polite "Buenos días" or "Buenas tardes."

- **Tipping**: Most restaurants include a 10% service charge on the bill, but it's common to leave an additional 5-10% tip if the service was excellent. In casual eateries and cafes, rounding up the bill is appreciated.

- **Pace of Dining:** Meals in the Dominican Republic, especially lunch, are often leisurely. Take your time and enjoy the experience. Don't be surprised if service is a bit slower than you're used to—this is part of the relaxed pace of life here.
- **Water and Drinks:** In many local restaurants, it's best to order bottled water to avoid any stomach troubles, as tap water is generally not recommended for tourists.

Exploring Dominican cuisine is a journey that takes you beyond the plate and into the heart of the island's rich history and traditions. From bustling food markets to charming local eateries, every meal tells a story—one that invites you to savor the Dominican way of life, one bite at a time.

Dominican Republic Travel Guide 2025

CHAPTER 9: NIGHTLIFE AND ENTERTAINMENT

When the sun sets in the Dominican Republic, the island comes alive with the rhythm of merengue, the sway of bachata, and the vibrant pulse of its nightlife. Whether you're seeking a lively club scene, intimate lounges, or live performances, there's something for everyone in the major cities. From the bustling streets of Santo Domingo to the laid-back beach town of Cabarete, the Dominican Republic offers a nightlife experience as diverse as its culture.

➢ Top Nightlife Spots

1. Santo Domingo: A City That Never Sleeps

As the capital, Santo Domingo is the heart of the island's nightlife scene. The city has it all—from chic rooftop bars with stunning views of the Caribbean Sea to electrifying dance clubs where merengue beats carry on until the early hours of the morning.

- **El Sartén "La Catedral de la Música Caribeña"**

Tucked away in the Zona Colonial, El Sartén is a hidden gem for those who prefer a more intimate setting. This cozy bar serves up excellent cocktails and frequently features live bands playing merengue and jazz. The colonial-era ambiance makes it perfect for a laid-back night with a touch of history.

SCAN TO ACCESS EL SARTÉN "LA CATEDRAL DE LA MÚSICA CARIBEÑA"

Address: Calle Hostos 153, Santo Domingo, Dominican Republic.
Contact Info: +1 829-763-6888

Dominican Republic Travel Guide 2025

Getting There: A 10-minute walk from most hotels in the Zona Colonial or a 5-minute taxi ride.

Local Tip: Head here on Fridays when local jazz musicians take the stage. It's less crowded than the bigger venues, giving you a more authentic, laid-back vibe.

- **Onno's Zona Colonial Bar & Restaurant**

For a combination of eating, drinking, and partying, Onno's Bar in the Zona Colonial is a top spot. Known for its lively atmosphere and outdoor dance floor, this bar is popular for its themed party nights and live music. It's a more casual spot where you can enjoy Dominican rum cocktails and even catch live sports.

SCAN TO ACCESS ONNO'S ZONA COLONIAL BAR & RESTAURANT

Dominican Republic Travel Guide 2025

Location: C. Hostos #157, Santo Domingo 10210, Dominican Republic

Local Tip: The outdoor area gets lively after 10 PM, so head over early for drinks and stay for the dancing.

- **VIP Room Santo Domingo**

For those looking for a more upscale experience, the VIP Room is a glamorous club located in the Piantini neighborhood. This venue offers a high-end party atmosphere, with a luxurious interior, private lounges, and a laser-lit dance floor. It's a go-to spot for fashionable locals and tourists alike.

SCAN TO ACCESS VIP ROOM SANTO DOMINGO

Location: Av. Abraham Lincoln 152, Santo Domingo 10148, Dominican Republic

Contact Info: +1 809-456-4523

Dominican Republic Travel Guide 2025

Local Tip: Dress to impress, as there's a strict dress code, and expect to pay a cover charge to access the VIP areas.

2. Cabarete: Beachfront Party Vibes

On the north coast, Cabarete is famous for its laid-back, beachfront nightlife. The town's strip of sandy bars and clubs offers a unique experience, where dancing barefoot under the stars is the norm.

- **Mojito Bar**

For a more relaxed vibe, Mojito Bar is the perfect beachfront spot in the downtown area. Known for its great cocktails and casual atmosphere, it's ideal for those who want to enjoy a few drinks with friends while listening to mellow tunes.

SCAN TO ACCESS MOJITO BAR

Dominican Republic Travel Guide 2025

Location: QH2V+5H8, Cabarete 57000, Dominican Republic

Contact Info: +1 809-571-9327

Local Tip: Go for happy hour to enjoy some of the best mojitos on the beach.

- **La Chabola**

A must-visit for live music lovers, La Chabola offers open mic nights on Wednesdays, where locals and expats come together to perform. The cozy, intimate setting is perfect for enjoying live acoustic sets with a cold drink in hand. It's known for its community atmosphere and reasonably priced drinks.

SCAN TO ACCESS LA CHABOLA

Location: 57000, Cabarete 57000, Dominican Republic

Contact Info: +1 809-543-5860

Local Tip: Try the pizza while you're there—many consider it one of the best in Cabarete.

➤Cultural Performances: Music, Theater, and Dance

The Dominican Republic's cultural scene extends far beyond the nightclubs, with live performances of traditional music, theater, and dance enriching the nightlife experience.

- **Teatro Nacional Eduardo Brito (Santo Domingo)**

This stunning theater in Santo Domingo's Plaza de la Cultura hosts a variety of cultural performances, from classical music concerts to contemporary Dominican plays. It's also home to the National Symphony Orchestra and frequently features ballet and opera performances.

Dominican Republic Travel Guide 2025

SCAN TO ACCESS TEATRO NACIONAL EDUARDO BRITO

Address: Av. Máximo Gómez 35, Santo Domingo 10204, Dominican Republic

Contact Info: +1 809-687-3191

How to Book Tickets: Tickets are available at the theater's box office or online via local ticket vendors like Uepa Tickets. Prices range from $10 to $50 USD depending on the performance.

- **Casa de Teatro (Santo Domingo)**

For a more intimate cultural experience, Casa de Teatro in the Zona Colonial is a hub for local musicians and artists. It's one of the best spots to catch live merengue and jazz performances, as well as art exhibits.

Dominican Republic Travel Guide 2025

SCAN TO ACCESS CASA DE TEATRO

Address: C. Arzobispo Meriño 110, Santo Domingo 10210, Dominican Republic

Contact Info: +1 809-689-3430.

How to Book Tickets: Check their schedule online or call ahead for reservations. Most performances are affordable, with tickets ranging from $5 to $15 USD.

- **Centro Cultural Eduardo León Jimenes (Santiago)**

In Santiago, the Centro León is a cultural powerhouse. In addition to showcasing local art and history, the center hosts regular music and dance performances, including traditional bachata nights.

Dominican Republic Travel Guide 2025

SCAN TO ACCESS CENTRO CULTURAL EDUARDO LEÓN JIMENES

Address: Av. 27 de Febrero 146, Santiago de los Caballeros 51053, Dominican Republic

Contact Info: +1 809-582-2315

How to Book Tickets: Visit their website or purchase tickets directly at the venue. Prices start at $5 USD.

★ Insider Tips for a Night Out

- **Dress to Impress in the City**

In Santo Domingo's upscale clubs, people take their fashion seriously. Opt for smart casual attire—men should wear collared shirts, and women often wear dresses or elegant outfits. Flip-flops or overly casual wear might get you turned away at the door.

- **Beach Casual in Cabarete**

In Cabarete, the vibe is far more relaxed. You'll fit right in wearing flip-flops, casual beachwear, or even barefoot if you're partying on the sand.

- **Safety Tips**

Stick to well-lit, busy areas when out at night, especially in Santo Domingo. While the nightlife is generally safe, petty theft can happen in crowded areas. It's best to take registered taxis or use Uber to get around, particularly late at night. Also, avoid flashy jewelry or valuables, and keep an eye on your belongings.

- **Pace Yourself**

Dominican nightlife starts late, with most clubs and bars not getting busy until 11 PM or even midnight. The energy lasts until the early hours, so pace yourself if you plan to party all night.

Whether you're dancing the night away in a vibrant Santo Domingo club or sipping cocktails by the beach in Cabarete, the Dominican Republic's nightlife has something for everyone. With a mix of modern party spots, intimate local bars, and rich cultural performances, the island offers a nightlife experience that blends fun

Dominican Republic Travel Guide 2025

with a deep connection to its music, dance, and traditions. So put on your dancing shoes—or kick them off if you're in Cabarete—and get ready to experience the Dominican Republic after dark, where the party never seems to end.

Dominican Republic Travel Guide 2025

CHAPTER 10: SHOPPING

Shopping in the Dominican Republic is a journey through both modern convenience and rich local tradition. Whether you're strolling through high-end malls or bargaining at vibrant local markets, the island offers a variety of shopping experiences to suit every taste. From artisanal crafts to world-renowned cigars and rum, there's something for every traveler looking to bring a piece of the island home. Here's your guide to the best shopping districts, tips for navigating markets, and where to find authentic, high-quality souvenirs.

Dominican Republic Travel Guide 2025

➤Best Shopping Districts: From High-End Malls to Local Markets

- **BlueMall (Santo Domingo and Punta Cana)**

If you're looking for high-end shopping, BlueMall is the place to be. With locations in both Santo Domingo and Punta Cana, it offers a range of luxury brands such as Louis Vuitton, Cartier, and Prada, alongside popular international retailers like Zara and Guess. It's a one-stop shop for those who prefer a sleek, modern shopping experience.

SCAN TO ACCESS BLUEMALL SANTO DOMINGO

Getting There in Santo Domingo:

Dominican Republic Travel Guide 2025

By Taxi or Uber: A 15-minute taxi ride from the Zona Colonial will get you to BlueMall, costing about $6-8 USD.

Location: Av. Winston Churchill 95, Santo Domingo, Dominican Republic

Contact Info: +1 809-955-3000

By Public Transport: Take the Metro Line 1 to the Pedro Henríquez Ureña stop, then it's a short 10-minute walk to the mall.

SCAN TO ACCESS BLUEMALL PUNTACANA

Getting There in Punta Cana:

By Taxi: From most Punta Cana resorts, it's a 20-30 minute taxi ride costing about $15-20 USD. Ask your hotel concierge to arrange transport.

Location: Blvd. Turístico del Este, Punta Cana 23000, Dominican Republic

Dominican Republic Travel Guide 2025

Contact Info: +1 809-784-4001

- **Plaza Lama (Santiago)**

Plaza Lama is a well-known department store chain in the Dominican Republic, and its Santiago location is one of the best places to shop for a variety of products. From fashion and electronics to home goods and groceries, Plaza Lama offers an extensive selection of local and international brands. This modern shopping experience is ideal for travelers looking for convenience and a wide range of products under one roof.

SCAN TO ACCESS PLAZA LAMA

Location: G597+P39, Carr. Mella, Santo Domingo Este, Dominican Republic

Contact Info: +1 809-701-5262

Getting There:

Dominican Republic Travel Guide 2025

Located in central Santiago, it's easily accessible by taxi from most major hotels and costs around $7-10 USD for a short ride.

Local Tip:

Check out their seasonal sales for great deals on clothing and electronics, especially during major holidays.

- **La Sirena**

A one-stop shopping experience, Multicentro La Sirena in La Romana is part supermarket, part department store. It offers everything from groceries to clothing and electronics. While not a traditional market, it's popular for visitors looking to grab essentials or shop for Dominican products like coffee and local art.

SCAN TO ACCESS LA SIRENA

Dominican Republic Travel Guide 2025

Getting There: Located in the center of La Romana, taxis from the hotel areas cost around $10 USD.

Location: Av. 14 de Junio Multiplaza La Romana Av. Circunvalación esquina Autopista del Este, La Romana 22000, Dominican Republic

Contact Info: +1 809-556-4446

Local Tip: Check for seasonal discounts on Dominican products, which make great gifts.

How to Haggle:

In Dominican markets, bargaining is expected, but always be respectful. Start by offering 50-60% of the initial asking price and negotiate from there. A friendly attitude goes a long way—vendors appreciate politeness, and it can lead to better deals.

★ Top Souvenirs to Bring Home

1. Cigars

The Dominican Republic is one of the world's largest producers of premium cigars, rivaling even Cuba. Look for brands like Arturo Fuente or La Aurora when shopping for cigars. To ensure you're getting a genuine product, always purchase from reputable stores or cigar factories.

How to Recognize Quality:

A high-quality cigar will feel firm but not hard when gently pressed. The wrapper should be smooth, with no cracks or blemishes. Also, make sure the cigars are kept in a proper humidor to preserve their freshness.

Where to Buy:

- **Tabacalera de García (La Romana):** For an immersive experience, visit the Tabacalera de García factory, the largest premium cigar factory in the world. You can tour the facility and purchase cigars directly from the source.

SCAN TO ACCESS TABACALERA DE GARCÍA

Location: La Romana 22000, Dominican Republic
Contact Info: +1 809-556-1555

Dominican Republic Travel Guide 2025

2. Dominican Rum

No visit to the Dominican Republic is complete without taking home a bottle of its famous rum. The island produces some of the best rums in the Caribbean, with Brugal, Barceló, and Ron Bermúdez being the most iconic brands.

How to Recognize Quality:
Look for aged rum, which will have a richer flavor profile. Dominican rum is known for its smoothness, often with notes of vanilla, caramel, and spices. Check the label for the rum's age—anything labeled "Añejo" or "Gran Añejo" will have been aged for several years.

Where to Buy:
Super Pola (various locations): A well-known supermarket chain where you can find a wide selection of Dominican rum at competitive prices.

La Sirena (nationwide): This large department store is perfect for grabbing a bottle of high-quality rum to bring home, often offering deals on popular brands.

3. Larimar Jewelry

Unique to the Dominican Republic, larimar is a stunning blue gemstone that makes for an unforgettable souvenir. Found only in the Dominican mountains, this rare stone is used to create beautiful pendants, rings, and bracelets.

How to Recognize Quality:

The most prized larimar has a deep, vibrant blue color. Be cautious of overly pale or white stones, as these are often lower quality. If you're purchasing high-end pieces, ask for a certificate of authenticity to ensure you're getting genuine larimar.

Where to Buy:

- **Ambar y Larimar Museum** (Santo Domingo): This museum offers a wide selection of high-quality larimar and amber jewelry, along with information about the stones' history and significance.

Dominican Republic Travel Guide 2025

SCAN TO ACCESS AMBAR Y LARIMAR MUSEUM

Location: C. Arzobispo Meriño 452, esq, Santo Domingo 10210, Dominican Republic

Contact Info: +1 809-682-3309

- **La Casa del Larimar** (Barahona): Located near the larimar mines, this small factory offers direct sales of handcrafted larimar jewelry, providing an opportunity to purchase at lower prices.

SCAN TO ACCESS LA CASA DEL LARIMAR

Location: Barahona 81000, Dominican Republic

Dominican Republic Travel Guide 2025

Supporting Local Artisans: Best Stores and Cooperatives

For travelers looking to support local communities, shopping at artisan cooperatives is a meaningful way to contribute to the local economy while bringing home unique, handmade treasures.

- **Arte Cuseco (Punta Cana)**

This artisan cooperative sells handcrafted goods made by local artists, including wood carvings, pottery, and intricate basketry. Each purchase helps sustain the local craftspeople and preserves traditional Dominican art forms.

Dominican Republic Travel Guide 2025

Location: C5X8+4RC, San Rafael del Yuma 23000, Dominican Republic

Getting There:

Located in the Punta Cana Village near the airport, it's an easy 10-minute taxi ride from most Punta Cana resorts.

Local Tip:

Look for items that showcase the unique craftsmanship of the region, especially hand-painted pottery and organic textiles.

- **Taíno Arte (La Vega)**

Located in La Vega, Taíno Art offers a range of handmade crafts that reflect the rich cultural heritage of the Dominican Republic. The store specializes in Taíno-inspired art, including wood carvings, pottery, and paintings, all crafted by local artisans. This shop is a must-visit for anyone looking to support local artists while purchasing unique and culturally significant souvenirs.

Dominican Republic Travel Guide 2025

SCAN TO ACCESS TAINO ARTE

Location: Autop. Juan Pablo Duarte km 15, La Vega 41000, Dominican Republic

Contact Info: +1 809-631-0584

Getting There:

Situated along Autop. Juan Pablo Duarte km 15, Taíno Art is a short drive from the city center of La Vega and accessible by taxi or rental car.

Local Tip:

Don't hesitate to ask the shop staff about the origins of the pieces—they're very knowledgeable and passionate about the cultural significance behind the artwork.

Whether you're seeking luxury shopping at modern malls or hunting for authentic Dominican treasures in bustling

Dominican Republic Travel Guide 2025

local markets, the Dominican Republic offers a rich and diverse shopping experience. From high-quality cigars and rum to stunning larimar jewelry, there's no shortage of unique souvenirs to bring home. Remember to haggle politely in markets, support local artisans, and savor the opportunity to connect with the Dominican Republic's vibrant culture through its crafts and goods.

Dominican Republic Travel Guide 2025

CHAPTER 11: SUGGESTED ITINERARIES

Whether you're visiting the Dominican Republic for a quick getaway or an extended stay, this island offers an array of experiences that cater to all types of travelers. From the historic streets of Santo Domingo to the tranquil beaches of Punta Cana, each itinerary highlights must-see attractions while providing transportation details and tips for relaxed versus fast-paced travel.

3-Day Itinerary: The Quick Getaway

Day 1: Explore Santo Domingo's Colonial Past

Morning: Start your trip in the Zona Colonial, a UNESCO World Heritage site in the heart of Santo Domingo. Wander through the cobblestone streets and visit landmarks like the Catedral Primada de Américas.

Dominican Republic Travel Guide 2025

Getting There: Stay in a hotel within the Zona Colonial so you can explore by foot.

Local Tip: Stop for lunch at Pat'e Palo, a popular restaurant in Plaza de España, and enjoy local dishes like Chicharrón de Pollo (fried chicken).

Afternoon: Visit the Museo de las Casas Reales and the nearby Fortaleza Ozama, both key sites in understanding the country's colonial history.

Transportation: The entire Zona Colonial is walkable, but you can easily take a short 5-minute taxi ride between landmarks if you prefer.

Evening: Cap off the day with dinner at Adrián Tropical, where you can sample authentic Dominican cuisine while enjoying views of the Caribbean Sea.

Day 2: Adventure in the Mountains of Jarabacoa

Morning: Head to Jarabacoa, the island's eco-tourism hub, known for its rivers and waterfalls. Take an early

Dominican Republic Travel Guide 2025

morning bus from Santo Domingo's Expreso Vegano station (3-hour ride, $8 USD).

Must-See: Salto de Jimenoa waterfall is a must. You can hike to the falls in about 45 minutes and enjoy the surrounding nature.

Afternoon: If you're feeling adventurous, try river rafting on the **Yaque del River**, the longest river in the Caribbean. Book through local companies like Rancho Baiguate.

Transportation: Local taxis or moto-taxis are available to take you from your hotel to the rafting base or waterfall hikes.

Evening: Relax in one of Jarabacoa's eco-lodges for a serene end to your day. Most lodges, like Rancho Baiguate, offer dinner as part of their stay.

Day 3: Beach Day in Punta Cana

Morning: Take an early flight or drive from Santiago to Punta Cana (45-minute flight or 4-hour drive). Start your

Dominican Republic Travel Guide 2025

day at Playa Bávaro, one of the most beautiful beaches in the Dominican Republic.

Transportation: Taxis or Uber from your accommodation can take you to the beach for around $15 USD.

Afternoon: Spend the afternoon relaxing on the beach or indulge in water sports like snorkeling or parasailing.

Local Tip: Grab lunch at La Yola, a seafood restaurant located in the Punta Cana Resort & Club with stunning views of the marina.

Evening: Fly out or spend the night in Punta Cana before heading home.

5-Day Itinerary: Classic Dominican Experience

Day 1 & 2: Discover Santo Domingo and Its Surroundings
Follow the Day 1 of the 3-day itinerary for a deep dive into Santo Domingo's rich history.

Dominican Republic Travel Guide 2025

On Day 2, venture to **Los Tres Ojos**, a series of crystal-clear caves just outside Santo Domingo. Take a guided tour to explore the underground lagoons.

Getting There: A 15-minute taxi ride from the Zona Colonial ($5-7 USD).

Day 3: Samaná's Natural Wonders

Morning: Travel to the Samaná Peninsula by car or bus (3-hour drive or bus ride from Santo Domingo, $15 USD). This is a paradise for eco-tourists and those seeking adventure.

Must-See: Take a boat tour of Los Haitises National Park, famous for its mangroves, caves, and birdwatching.

Afternoon: Visit **Playa Rincón**, a secluded, pristine beach considered one of the most beautiful in the world.

Dominican Republic Travel Guide 2025

Getting There: A 45-minute drive from Samaná town or hire a local boat taxi from Las Galeras.

Local Tip: Enjoy fresh seafood at one of the beachside shacks.

Day 4 & 5: Punta Cana Relaxation and Water Sports
Morning: Fly or drive to Punta Cana and spend the day at **Playa Macao**, a more secluded alternative to Bávaro Beach, perfect for surfing.

Local Tip: Arrange a surf lesson through local schools for $25 USD.

Afternoon: For a more relaxed experience, head to Indigenous Eyes Ecological Reserve, a hidden gem where you can hike and swim in natural lagoons.

Getting There: A 15-minute taxi ride from Punta Cana Resort.

Dominican Republic Travel Guide 2025

Evening: End your trip with a sunset dinner at La Palapa in the Eden Roc Cap Cana Resort.

7-Day Itinerary: A True Island Explorer's Journey

Day 1 & 2: Santo Domingo's History and Culture
Follow Day 1 & 2 of the 5-day itinerary, with additional time to explore museums and local markets like Mercado Modelo, where you can haggle for souvenirs such as Larimar jewelry and Dominican cigars.

Day 3 & 4: The Mountain Town of Jarabacoa
Take a break from the beaches and immerse yourself in the lush greenery of Jarabacoa.

Must-Do: On Day 3, take a guided hike up to Pico Duarte, the highest peak in the Caribbean. For a less strenuous activity, opt for horseback riding through the mountain trails.

Day 4: Visit El Limón Waterfall, where you can swim in the refreshing pools at the base of the falls.

Dominican Republic Travel Guide 2025

Transportation: From Santo Domingo, you can either rent a car (3-hour drive) or take a bus ($8 USD) to Jarabacoa.

Day 5 & 6: Samaná's Whales and Beaches

Day 5: If visiting between January and March, don't miss whale watching in Samaná Bay. This region is one of the best places in the world to see humpback whales.

Day 6: Spend the day at Playa Rincón, or for something even more secluded, visit Playa Frontón by boat.

Transportation: From Samaná, most tours and boat trips can be arranged through local operators. The easiest way to get to these beaches is by boat taxi.

Day 7: Farewell in Punta Cana

Morning: Finish your journey with a relaxing morning on Playa Bávaro, where you can soak up the sun or enjoy a final swim in the crystal-clear waters.

Dominican Republic Travel Guide 2025

Afternoon: Take in one last seafood meal at a beachfront restaurant before flying out of Punta Cana International Airport.

Alternative Routes for Relaxed vs. Fast-Paced Travel

Relaxed Itinerary: Focus more on fewer destinations. If you prefer a slower pace, spend additional nights in each location (Santo Domingo, Jarabacoa, and Punta Cana). This allows you to fully immerse yourself in local culture without rushing between attractions.

For example, instead of covering both Santo Domingo and Samaná, spend your entire stay in Santo Domingo and its surrounding areas, enjoying extended visits to beaches and historical sites.

Fast-Paced Itinerary: If you're eager to experience as much as possible, opt for domestic flights between Santo Domingo, Samaná, and Punta Cana to save time and maximize your sightseeing. Prioritize must-see attractions like Los Haitises National Park and whale watching, but move quickly between destinations to fit everything in.

With these itineraries, you can experience the Dominican Republic at your own pace, whether you're in for a whirlwind adventure or a more leisurely escape. From the vibrant streets of Santo Domingo to the tranquil beaches of Punta Cana, there's something here for every kind of traveler.

➢Hidden Gems of the Dominican Republic

While the Dominican Republic is well-known for its popular tourist spots like Punta Cana and Santo Domingo, it's the lesser-known destinations that offer a more authentic and enriching experience. Venture off the beaten path, and you'll discover hidden beaches, charming villages, and local treasures that will give you a deeper connection to the island's culture and natural beauty.

Dominican Republic Travel Guide 2025

These hidden gems provide a glimpse into the quieter side of the Dominican Republic, perfect for travelers looking to escape the crowds while still enjoying all that this Caribbean paradise has to offer.

1. Playa Frontón (Samaná Peninsula)

Situated at the base of dramatic cliffs, Playa Frontón is one of the most secluded beaches in the Dominican Republic. Accessible only by boat or a challenging hike, this beach is a hidden paradise with pristine waters perfect for snorkeling and a shoreline fringed by coconut trees. The lack of crowds makes it an ideal spot for travelers seeking solitude and natural beauty.

Dominican Republic Travel Guide 2025

| SCAN TO ACCESS PLAYA FRONTÓN | [QR code] |

Getting There:

From Las Galeras: Take a boat taxi from Las Galeras, which costs around $30 USD round trip and takes 20-30 minutes. Alternatively, for the adventurous, there is a 3-hour hike through jungle paths starting from Las Galeras.

Local Tip: Hire a local guide in Las Galeras if you choose to hike, as the trail can be tricky to navigate.

What to Do:

Bring snorkeling gear to explore the vibrant coral reefs just offshore, or simply relax on the quiet sands with nothing but the sound of the waves.

Pack your own food and water as there are no facilities on this remote beach.

2. Barahona: The Unspoiled Southwest

For travelers looking to experience an entirely different side of the Dominican Republic, Barahona is a gem that remains untouched by mass tourism. This southwestern region is home to rugged mountains, sparkling blue rivers, and remote beaches, offering a raw and authentic experience. The area's natural beauty includes the Bahía de las Águilas, considered by many to be the most beautiful beach in the country, and Lago Enriquillo, a hypersaline lake inhabited by crocodiles and flamingos.

Getting There:

From Santo Domingo: Barahona is a 3-hour drive from Santo Domingo via the Autopista 6 de Noviembre. Renting a car is the best way to explore the area at your own pace.

Local Tip: For safety, it's best to drive during daylight hours, as the roads can be narrow and winding in some parts.

Must-See Sights:

Dominican Republic Travel Guide 2025

- **Bahía de las Águilas:** This untouched beach is accessible by boat from the nearby town of Pedernales, about a 2-hour drive from Barahona. Its clear waters and isolated shores make it perfect for a day of swimming and relaxation.
- **Lago Enriquillo**: A visit to this unique saltwater lake, located about 45 minutes from Barahona, offers a chance to see wildlife like iguanas, flamingos, and American crocodiles. There are guided boat tours available for closer wildlife observation.

Local Tip:
For an authentic meal, stop by a family-owned restaurant like Comedor Mary in Barahona, where you can enjoy fresh, home-cooked Dominican dishes like Pescado con Coco (fish in coconut sauce) for less than $10 USD.

3. **Jarabacoa: Mountain Adventures in the Heart of the Island**

Dominican Republic Travel Guide 2025

Located in the mountains of the Dominican Republic's central highlands, Jarabacoa is a hidden gem for adventure travelers. Known for its cooler climate and lush landscapes, Jarabacoa offers stunning waterfalls, hiking trails, and river rafting. This quiet mountain town is ideal for those looking to escape the beach crowds and immerse themselves in nature.

Getting There:
From Santo Domingo or Santiago: Jarabacoa is about a 2-hour drive from Santo Domingo and just 1 hour from Santiago. The most convenient way to travel is by car, though buses run from Santo Domingo's Expreso Vegano station for around $8 USD.

What to Do:
Salto Jimenoa Two: This waterfall is a must-see, and you can reach it by a short hike through the surrounding rainforest. It's a great spot for cooling off with a swim.

Pico Duarte Hike: If you're feeling adventurous, take on the challenge of hiking Pico Duarte, the highest peak in the Caribbean. A multi-day guided trek will take you through the island's most scenic highland terrain.

Local Tip:

Stay at an eco-lodge like Jarabacoa River Club, where you can wake up to the sound of the rushing river and enjoy farm-to-table meals prepared by local chefs. The lodges here prioritize sustainability and conservation efforts, making them an eco-friendly option for travelers.

4. Constanza: The Hidden Valley

Often referred to as the Switzerland of the Caribbean, Constanza is a valley town surrounded by towering mountains, fertile farmlands, and cool breezes. At an elevation of over 1,200 meters, it offers a refreshing change from the island's tropical heat. Constanza is known for its fresh produce, including strawberries, avocados, and flowers, making it a beautiful and tranquil escape for those seeking a slower pace.

Getting There:

From Santiago or Santo Domingo: Constanza is a 2-hour drive from Santiago and about 3 hours from Santo Domingo. A car is essential for navigating the mountainous roads, though buses and public transportation are available from larger cities.

Local Tip: The drive to Constanza offers scenic mountain views, so plan a few stops along the way to enjoy the landscape.

What to Do:

- **Reserva Científica Ebano Verde**: This lush nature reserve offers miles of hiking trails through cloud forests, with opportunities to spot endemic species of birds and plants.

- **Aguas Blancas Waterfall:** This stunning waterfall, one of the highest in the Caribbean, is just a short drive from the center of Constanza. A dip in the icy water is a refreshing treat after a hike.

Local Tip:

Stop by Granja D'Señor Pepe, a local farm that offers tours and tastings of organic strawberries and other fresh produce. You can also buy homemade jams and other local delicacies to take home as souvenirs.

★ Tips for Finding Hidden Gems

- **Talk to Locals**

One of the best ways to find hidden gems is by asking locals for their recommendations. Whether it's your taxi driver, hotel staff, or someone you meet at a restaurant, Dominicans are friendly and eager to share their favorite spots with visitors.

- **Avoid Peak Tourist Seasons**

For a more relaxed experience, plan your visit during the off-season (May to November). You'll find fewer crowds at even the most popular attractions, and locals will have more time to share their insider tips with you.

- **Stay in Family-Run Guesthouses**

Instead of large resorts, opt for family-owned guesthouses or boutique hotels. These accommodations not only offer a more personalized experience but are also located in lesser-known areas that many tourists overlook.

Recommendations for Safe Off-the-Beaten-Path Travel

- **Stay Connected:** While exploring more remote areas, it's important to keep in touch with family or friends and let them know your travel plans. Consider buying a local SIM card for access to GPS and emergency services.
- **Travel During Daylight**: If driving to remote areas like Barahona or Constanza, try to complete your journey during daylight hours. Road conditions can be tricky, and some areas may lack proper lighting.
- **Hire Local Guides:** For hikes, boat tours, or visits to lesser-known areas, it's always safer and more enjoyable to go with a local guide who knows the terrain and can share insights into the region's culture and history.

Dominican Republic Travel Guide 2025

By exploring these hidden gems, you'll experience the Dominican Republic in its most authentic and untouched form. Whether it's a hike through the cool highlands of Constanza, a secluded beach in Samaná, or a rustic meal at a family-run restaurant, these off-the-beaten-path destinations offer unforgettable adventures for the intrepid traveler.

Dominican Republic Travel Guide 2025

CHAPTER 12: STAYING SAFE AND HEALTHY

The Dominican Republic is a beautiful and welcoming country, but like any popular destination, it's important to be mindful of safety and health. Whether you're a solo traveler, visiting with family, or exploring the island with friends, taking a few precautions will ensure that your trip is not only enjoyable but also safe. Here's what you need to know about avoiding common tourist scams, staying healthy in the tropical climate, and navigating local healthcare.

Common Tourist Scams and How to Avoid Them

While most visits to the Dominican Republic are trouble-free, there are a few common scams that tourists should be aware of:

- **The "Broken Meter" Taxi Scam**

In some cases, taxi drivers may claim their meter is broken or simply not use it. As a result, they charge inflated rates at the end of the trip.

How to Avoid It: Always agree on a price before getting into the taxi or opt for a reputable ride-sharing service like Uber, which operates in major cities like Santo Domingo and Punta Cana. Alternatively, you can request your hotel or restaurant to call a trusted taxi service.

- **"Helpful" Strangers at ATMs**

Dominican Republic Travel Guide 2025

Occasionally, individuals may offer to "help" tourists use an ATM and then either overcharge them for the assistance or steal their card details.

How to Avoid It: Only use ATMs located inside banks, and always be cautious when withdrawing cash. Politely decline any offers of assistance.

- **Fake Tour Operators**

Some travelers report being sold overpriced or non-existent tours by unauthorized street vendors.

How to Avoid It: Book tours through your hotel or well-established tour agencies. If you're buying a tour independently, research the company online and read reviews to ensure its legitimacy.

Safest Areas to Stay and Travel

While the Dominican Republic is generally safe for tourists, it's always a good idea to stick to well-known areas, particularly if you're traveling solo or with children.

- **Punta Cana**

The Punta Cana area is one of the safest and most popular regions for tourists. It's home to numerous resorts, all-inclusive hotels, and plenty of activities designed with visitors in mind. This region has a heavy police presence and most tourist areas are secure.

- **Samaná Peninsula**

The Samaná Peninsula is another safe area, known for its ecotourism, whale watching, and stunning beaches. While it's more remote, it's perfect for travelers looking for a peaceful, nature-filled escape.

- **Zona Colonial, Santo Domingo**

The Zona Colonial in Santo Domingo is a well-patrolled, tourist-friendly area where you can walk through the historic streets and visit important landmarks. As always in larger cities, be mindful of your belongings and avoid walking alone late at night in less populated areas.

★ Health Tips for Coping with the Tropical Climate

The Dominican Republic's tropical climate can be beautiful but challenging, especially if you're not used to the heat and humidity. Here are a few health tips to help you stay comfortable:

- **Stay Hydrated**

With temperatures often soaring above 30°C (86°F), staying hydrated is crucial. Drink plenty of water, but make sure it's bottled or purified. Avoid tap water, and even be cautious with ice in drinks if you're unsure of its source.

- **Sun Protection**

The sun is strong year-round, so make sure to wear sunscreen with at least SPF 30, and reapply every two hours, especially if you're swimming or sweating. Wearing a hat and light, breathable clothing can help protect you from sunburn.

- **Stay Cool**

Take breaks in the shade or air-conditioned spaces to avoid overheating, especially during the hottest part of the day (midday to early afternoon). Plan outdoor activities for the early morning or late afternoon when temperatures are cooler.

- **Mosquito Protection**

Mosquitoes can carry diseases like dengue or chikungunya, so use insect repellent (preferably one containing DEET) and wear long sleeves and pants, especially in rural or wooded areas.

Guide to Local Healthcare Facilities and Pharmacies

If you find yourself in need of medical assistance while traveling, rest assured that the Dominican Republic has modern healthcare facilities in most tourist areas.

1. **Hospitals and Clinics**
   - **Santo Domingo**: The capital city has several reputable private hospitals, such as Hospital General de la Plaza de la Salud and Centro Médico Punta Cana. Both offer high-quality care, including English-speaking staff for international visitors.

Dominican Republic Travel Guide 2025

Location 1: Av. José Ortega y Gasset, Santo Domingo, Dominican Republic

Contact Info: +1 809-565-7477

SCAN TO ACCESS HOSPITAL GENERAL DE LA PLAZA DE LA SALUD

Location 2: Av. España No.1, Punta Cana 23000, Dominican Republic

Contact Info: +1 809-552-1506

SCAN TO ACCESS CENTRO MÉDICO PUNTA CANA

- **Punta Cana**: The Hospiten Bavaro in Punta Cana is a modern private hospital known for

Dominican Republic Travel Guide 2025

treating tourists. It offers emergency services and has an international patient department.

SCAN TO ACCESS HOSPITEN BÁVARO

Location: Carretera Verón - Punta Cana,106, Punta Cana 23000, Dominican Republic
Contact Info: +1 809-686-1414

- **Santiago:** HOMS Hospital in Santiago is one of the top medical facilities in the Caribbean, offering a full range of services.

Location: Autop. Juan Pablo Duarte Km. 28, Santiago de los Caballeros 51000, Dominican Republic
Contact Info: +1 829-947-2222

Dominican Republic Travel Guide 2025

SCAN TO ACCESS HOMS HOSPITAL

2. Pharmacies

Pharmacies, or farmacias, are easy to find in most cities. Farmax and Caribbean Pharmacy are popular chains that carry a wide range of over-the-counter medications, including pain relievers, antihistamines, and sunscreen. Many larger pharmacies have English-speaking staff.

Local Tip: If you're staying in a remote area, stock up on essential medications before you go, as pharmacies can be limited outside of major cities and tourist areas.

3. Emergency Numbers

General Emergency (Police, Fire, Ambulance): Dial 911. Tourist Police (Politur): (809) 200-3500. They are specifically trained to assist visitors.

Traveling with Children or as a Solo Traveler

Whether you're traveling solo or with kids, taking extra precautions can ensure a safe and smooth journey.

1. **For Solo Travelers**

Stay in Safe, Central Areas: Opt for accommodations in safe neighborhoods such as the Zona Colonial in Santo Domingo or near popular resorts in Punta Cana. Staying in tourist areas reduces the likelihood of encountering unsafe situations.

- **Blend In:** Avoid flashing expensive jewelry or gadgets, as this can make you a target for pickpocketing. Dress modestly and confidently, as this can help you blend in with locals.
- **Stay Connected**: Always have a charged phone and, if possible, buy a local SIM card for easy communication and access to maps. Let someone back home know your travel plans.

2. **Traveling with Children**

Family-Friendly Accommodations: Stick to all-inclusive resorts in Punta Cana, Puerto Plata, or La Romana, which offer child-friendly amenities like kids' clubs, family rooms, and pools.

- **Beach Safety:** While the Dominican Republic's beaches are beautiful, always keep an eye on your children when they're near the water. Some beaches, like Playa Bávaro, have calm waters, but others can have strong currents.
- **Medical Kit**: Carry a travel-sized first-aid kit with essentials like bandages, antiseptic wipes, and medication for common issues like motion sickness or allergies.

By staying aware of potential scams, preparing for the tropical climate, and knowing where to find local healthcare facilities, you can enjoy your time in the Dominican Republic with peace of mind. Whether you're adventuring solo or with your family, the island offers both excitement and tranquility, all while maintaining a focus on safety.

Dominican Republic Travel Guide 2025

CHAPTER 13: LEAVING THE DOMINICAN REPUBLIC

As your time in the Dominican Republic comes to an end, it's important to plan ahead for a smooth departure. Whether you're traveling from Santo Domingo, Punta Cana, or other popular destinations, here's your step-by-step guide to getting to the airport, navigating customs, and handling last-minute travel logistics.

Step-by-Step Directions for Getting to the Airport

1. **From Santo Domingo to Las Américas International Airport (SDQ)**

Las Américas International Airport is about 30 kilometers (19 miles) east of downtown Santo Domingo.

By Taxi or Uber: The easiest way to get to the airport is by taxi or Uber. A taxi ride from the Zona Colonial will take about 30-45 minutes, depending on traffic, and will cost around $25-30 USD. Uber is usually a bit cheaper, averaging $15-20 USD for the same route.

By Private Transfer: If you're traveling with a group or have a lot of luggage, booking a private transfer through your hotel or a local service is convenient. Prices start at $35 USD.

By Bus: Public buses, known as guaguas, are available but not recommended if you have a lot of luggage. The Express Boca Chica bus stops near the airport, costing $1 USD, but you'll need a taxi or ride-share from the stop to the airport terminal.

2. From Punta Cana to Punta Cana International Airport (PUJ)

Punta Cana International Airport is the primary gateway for tourists flying in and out of the region, conveniently located near major resorts.

By Taxi or Uber: The quickest and most reliable way to get to the airport is by taxi. From the Bávaro or Cap

Dominican Republic Travel Guide 2025

Cana areas, it's about a 20-minute drive and costs approximately $20-30 USD. Uber operates in Punta Cana but is less common than in Santo Domingo, with prices ranging from $10-20 USD.

By Hotel Shuttle: Many all-inclusive resorts offer free or low-cost shuttle services to the airport. Check with your hotel's front desk to confirm availability and departure times.

3. From Puerto Plata to Gregorio Luperón International Airport (POP)

Gregorio Luperón International Airport serves the north coast of the Dominican Republic, about 15 kilometers (9 miles) from Puerto Plata.

By Taxi: A taxi ride from Puerto Plata to the airport takes around 20 minutes and costs $20-25 USD.

By Hotel Shuttle: Many hotels in Puerto Plata and nearby areas like Sosúa and Cabarete offer shuttle services. Check with your hotel for schedules and costs, as some may offer complimentary transfers.

4. From Samaná to El Catey International Airport (AZS)

For travelers in the Samaná Peninsula, El Catey International Airport is about 40 minutes from the town of Las Terrenas.

By Taxi or Private Transfer: A taxi from Las Terrenas to the airport costs around $50 USD. For those staying in more remote parts of Samaná, expect to pay $70-100 USD for the ride.

Guide to the Customs Process and Duty-Free Shopping

1. Customs Process at Dominican Airports

The customs process at Dominican airports is straightforward, but being prepared will save you time and hassle:

Immigration: Upon arrival at the airport, you'll go through immigration where you'll present your passport and boarding pass. Make sure you have filled out the Dominican Republic e-ticket form (available online) before heading to the airport. This digital form consolidates immigration, customs, and health declaration into one step.

Customs: After passing through immigration, you'll collect your luggage and proceed to the customs area. Here, you may be asked to declare items if you are carrying high-value goods or large amounts of cash. Most tourists pass through without issues, as long as they follow standard rules (e.g., no fruits, plants, or significant sums of undeclared currency).

2. Duty-Free Shopping

Each of the Dominican Republic's international airports has a range of duty-free shops where you can purchase local products and international goods. Here's what to look out for:

- **Cigars and Rum**: The Dominican Republic is famous for both, and you can find great deals on

Dominican Republic Travel Guide 2025

premium cigars (like Arturo Fuente and La Flor Dominicana) and top-quality rum brands (Brugal, Barceló, Ron Bermúdez).

- **Jewelry**: For a truly Dominican souvenir, shop for larimar or amber jewelry at the duty-free shops. The prices are competitive, and you can often find certified pieces.

Perfumes, Liquor, and Cosmetics: Like most duty-free shops worldwide, Dominican airports offer discounts on international liquor, perfumes, and beauty products. Prices may be lower than what you'd find at home, but compare before you buy.

Duty-Free Allowance for Returning Home:

Before making purchases, be sure to check the duty-free allowances for your home country. For example, U.S. travelers can generally bring back 1 liter of alcohol, 200 cigarettes, and $800 worth of merchandise duty-free.

Dominican Republic Travel Guide 2025

★ Final Tips for Departure

1. Check Flight Status

Always check your flight status before heading to the airport. Most airlines allow you to check flight statuses on their apps or websites. Delays and gate changes are common, so it's good to stay updated. Also, aim to arrive at the airport 2-3 hours before your flight, especially if you're flying internationally.

2. Currency Exchange and Leftover Pesos

If you have any leftover Dominican pesos, you can exchange them for your home currency at the airport. However, airport exchange rates can be unfavorable, so if you have a chance, exchange your pesos at a local bank or exchange bureau before heading to the airport. Alternatively, use your pesos for last-minute purchases like souvenirs or food.

3. Last-Minute Logistics

Packing: Ensure your luggage meets your airline's weight and size limits to avoid any extra fees. Most

Dominican Republic Travel Guide 2025

international flights allow checked luggage up to 23 kg (50 lbs) and carry-on luggage with a weight limit of 7-10 kg (15-22 lbs).

Documents: Double-check that you have your passport, boarding pass, and travel insurance information easily accessible. Many airlines also now require proof of your vaccination status or a negative COVID test, depending on destination requirements.

4. Snacks and Water:

While there are plenty of dining options at Dominican airports, prices tend to be high. Grab a snack or drink from your hotel before you leave, and consider packing an empty water bottle to fill up after security.

5. Security Lines:

Be ready for airport security by having your liquids (under 100ml) and electronics easily accessible. Security lines can move slowly, especially during peak travel hours, so factor that into your timing.

Dominican Republic Travel Guide 2025

Departing the Dominican Republic can be just as smooth as your arrival with the right preparation. From selecting the best transportation options to knowing how to navigate customs and duty-free shopping, these tips will ensure that your final moments on the island are stress-free. Double-check your flight details, take care of last-minute logistics, and enjoy your final hours in this Caribbean paradise.

CONCLUSION

As we reach the end of this guide, I hope it has inspired you to enjoy the Dominican Republic in all its vibrant glory. From the sun-soaked beaches of Punta Cana to the bustling markets in Santo Domingo, this island is a rich mix of culture, natural beauty, and warm-hearted people. Whether you're lounging on a pristine beach, discovering hidden local treasures, or diving into the flavorful local cuisine, there's something here for every traveler.

The journey doesn't end with this guide—it's just the beginning. Take time to discover places that spark your interest and follow the rhythm of the island. You'll find that the Dominican Republic is not only about where you go but also how it makes you feel. From the lively streets of Santo Domingo to the quieter, off-the-beaten-path destinations like the artisan markets in Las Terrenas, every corner of this country holds something special.

Dominican Republic Travel Guide 2025

As you plan your next steps—whether it's navigating the best spots for nightlife, finding local crafts, or enjoying nature's beauty—remember that this guide is your companion. It's been designed to give you the tips and insights you need for a fulfilling trip, but it's your personal experiences that will make the journey unforgettable.

Safe travels, and enjoy every moment of your Dominican adventure. The memories you make here will stay with you long after the trip ends.

Dominican Republic Travel Guide 2025

NOTES

Dominican Republic Travel Guide 2025

Dominican Republic Travel Guide 2025

Dear Readers,

While every effort has been exerted to ensure the precision of this guide, the possibility of occasional errors or outdated information cannot be entirely dismissed. If you encounter any discrepancies, your input is highly valued. Please do not hesitate to contact me via email at conormcmillantravels@gmail.com. I am committed to incorporating any necessary corrections into forthcoming editions. Your feedback is invaluable in enhancing the quality of future editions and other publications under development.

Furthermore, if you have found this book to be beneficial, I would be immensely grateful if you could consider leaving a positive review and sharing it with others who may benefit from its contents. Your support is profoundly meaningful and contributes to the enhancement of future content for readers.

Thank you for your unwavering support and understanding.

Sincerely, Conor. S. McMillan

Printed in Great Britain
by Amazon